THE
TRANSFORMATION
ROADMAP

ACCELERATING ORGANISATION CHANGE

Paul Mooney

OAK·TREE·PRESS

OAK TREE PRESS
19 Rutland Street, Cork, Ireland
www.oaktreepress.com

A catalogue record of this book is
available from the British Library.

ISBN 978-1-78119-035-7 Paperback
ISBN 978-1-78119-036-4 ePub
ISBN 978-1-78119-037-1 Kindle

CONTENTS

FIGURES

ACKNOWLEDGEMENTS

Books are seldom the fruit of individual effort and several people have been involved in this construction.

The Clients: Firstly, an enormous "Thank You" is due to the client companies who, for 20+ years, have allowed me to experiment with a variety of approaches to managing change. Working as a management consultant is definitely one of the most interesting jobs in the world. I have had the opportunity to work on a range of complex organisational challenges and work with the best brains in the business! If all those change programmes seemed well worked out in advance, great. In reality, it was sometimes the science of muddling through. But the good news is that we did get through (most of the time, anyway). This book details your stories. Many of the clients are named directly in the book – a public acknowledgment of success in overcoming the myriad difficulties faced. In some cases, where the change efforts were less successful, names of organisations and individuals have been disguised to save blushes or future legal correspondence! In a small number of cases, I have changed company names and removed sensitive market or financial information – provided this did not materially affect the storyline. I really hope that clients will find this book a useful tool in managing future organisation change projects because one thing is certain: there will be future organisation change projects. It is the nature of the world you inhabit.

Tandem Team: The Tandem Consulting team jointly developed the model that provides the centrepiece of this book. We wanted to construct an approach to managing large-scale change projects that really works. In developing the model, we considered a variety of existing materials and sources. Earlier approaches we had developed were placed alongside well-known models like McKinsey's 7S. Eventually, after wading through some dense fog, the Transformation Roadmap emerged. A huge thanks to Cathy Buffini, Paul Dooley, Alex McDonnell, Cameron McDonnell, John O'Dowd, Dermot Rush and Jenny Smyth – for their expertise and endless patience as we battled through those debates. More than just co-developers of the model, this talented group have become friends as we have soldiered together on many of the cases in the pages that follow.

The Reviewers: Paul Dooley, Deirdre Giblin, Karl O'Connor, Dermot Rush and Catherine Whelan reviewed an earlier draft of the book and suggested a host of useful changes. The final product is much stronger as a result of their collective wisdom (perhaps I have discovered the secret to success: getting other people to make you look clever!).

Publisher: Grateful thanks to Brian O'Kane and the Oak Tree Press team for steering this project through the publication process and pretending that they enjoyed it!

Mooney Team: Linda, Amie, Cillian and Nicole put up with my physical and/or mental absence during the writing of this book. Sometimes, I think they even noticed that I wasn't there ...

To all of the above, grateful thanks and the usual absolution of responsibility for errors.

Paul Mooney
March 2012

1

INTRODUCTION

It is not the strongest of the species who survives, nor the most intelligent, but the one who is most adaptable to change.
Charles Darwin

The central goal in writing this book is to develop a practical approach to support line managers in navigating organisational change, a satnav for scoping and accelerating change projects. It provides an instruction booklet – a guide to moving your organisation from A (*today*) to B (*tomorrow*). Many books about managing change are directed at an academic audience, making it difficult to access the material,[1] while the opposite approach is taken sometimes by 'How To' books that detail individual steps without any insight into the underpinning theory. This is an attempt to bridge the gap between theory and practice. The book describes how change is managed in real organisational settings – based on an underpinning model of how effective organisations work. The model is grounded in our collective experience, both in Ireland and internationally, of managing hundreds of individual change projects across a range of commercial and not-for-profit sectors.

---

[1]   While I have drawn from the literature in the construction of this book, the core focus has been to guide clients in managing *real* projects. In the consulting world, we get paid for results (and get return work based on results achieved). While the science that underpins organisational change is interesting to some clients, most are more interested in solutions, rather than concepts. One USA client said that he did not want to hire a 'consultant' but wanted to work with a 'resultant', which captures this point.

Target Audience: The target audience for this book are managers who work at the coalface of improving performance. While the goal is to demystify the change process, it is important to stress that change is an inherently messy process. There is no escape from some confusion, regardless of how well the terrain is mapped. While the steps outlined in this book should reduce the fog, it cannot be completely eliminated.

Transformation Roadmap: Designing and implementing change programmes is a complex undertaking. Venturing into the unknown without a roadmap can lead to a condition known as 'getting lost'. *The Transformation Roadmap* provides the underpinning theory, a model of how all organisations work. An airport, a manufacturing operation, an international pharmaceutical company and a hospital all share common organisational elements. An understanding of these common elements is a precursor to managing change effectively. You cannot change an organisation unless you have a fundamental understanding of how it currently works and how you want it to work in the future. While this book will guide your efforts and increase the likelihood of success, the roadmap put forward is not an exact sequence of steps. Organisation change is a dynamic process that requires both pre-planning and constant mid-course correction as you work through the individual phases.

Irish Focus: The book has an important subsidiary goal. For many years, I have argued that Irish managers are overly reliant on organisational concepts and change models developed in other countries. While there are obvious similarities in the way all organisations work, there are also subtle cultural differences. Too few books are written that celebrate Irish success stories and are about managing an Irish workforce. An example may make this point clearer. Many years ago, I worked with General Electric in Ohio, where employees in the factory all wore T-shirts bearing the slogan: 'GE is me'. Irish executives seldom get the benefit of this level of personal identification with the organisation. The case studies peppered throughout the book demonstrate how to harness the humour (and cynicism) that is an integral part of the Irish culture.

One Journey – Three Stages: The book explores three stages that occur in all successful change journeys – developing an overall change strategy, choosing specific change targets and systematic change implementation.[2]

Overall Strategy:[3] Choosing the correct strategy to steer a change process is critical. In practice, there are several potential approaches to managing change – exactly the opposite of the 'one-best-way' mantra that many books put forward. The 'trick' is to choose the strategy that suits your particular organisation. During the planning phase, a key decision point is assessing organisational readiness. Successful change programmes kick-off with a solid managerial understanding of exactly what is required, from the launch phase through to the post-mortem. We review how to assess organisation readiness later in the book.

Change Targets: Assuming that you move beyond 'go', the second key element is the appropriate change levers – the specific areas selected for improvement. The critical issue here is getting the diagnosis right – that is, figuring out which levers offer breakthrough performance potential. We have witnessed many change programmes that identified the wrong issues – resulting in very limited performance improvement – lots of effort invested for a limited return. Choosing change targets that can deliver powerful productivity breakthroughs is critical. The book will guide you towards choosing key targets – sorting shark from minnow targets.[4]

Systematic Implementation: The final element in successful change programmes is to ensure that the implementation stage is managed clinically well. Typically, poor implementation is the Achilles' heel of change projects. The phrase 'Eventually, every great idea degenerates into donkey work' captures this brilliantly. To help ensure that this

---

2   In exploring individual topics, a layout conundrum comes to the fore. For example, staff engagement does not happen at a particular moment in time but is an ongoing feature across change management programmes. To keep some 'order' to the book, I have placed the topics in the most logical sequence, recognising that the specific topic also may come into play during other phases of the change cycle.

3   The terms used in the literature on Organisation Development can be confusing. Throughout, we have used the terms most commonly used.

4   You will be familiar with the phrase: 'Less is more'. This usually has good application to change programmes. I also like the Chinese proverb: 'When you chase two rabbits, you catch neither'.

work gets done, a clear implementation pathway is needed and we review a number of approaches to this. Under this heading, a key focus is on change *sustainability*. Organisations that undergo a period of change need to guard against a tendency to slide back into old practices. When the 'war room' is abandoned and the consultants have long since departed, managers need to ensure that changes remain in place by embedding a culture of continuous improvement. This acts as a ratchet mechanism, stopping organisations from sliding back into a pattern of underperformance.

Consulting Expertise: While the primary goal is to simplify the change process for practising managers, there is a huge element of self-interest in writing this book. While the Tandem Consulting team have been involved in hundreds of individual change projects, writing helps to sharpen our thinking about techniques that add real value. We have worked with dozens of change models and all sorts of planning tools. The Transformation Roadmap represents a stripped-down approach that is simple, but effective. It has been tested and refined in a variety of settings (for example, in the technology, manufacturing, financial services, pharmaceuticals and public service sectors). We know it works because we have the collective scars to prove it!

Overcoming Scepticism: To breathe life into the model, I have used actual case studies of both successful and unsuccessful change management projects. Nothing silences the sceptics on the sidelines like a goal in the back of the net. The hope is that the Transformation Roadmap will give you the personal confidence to tackle change projects within your organisation – learning from the lessons of others.

Client Empowerment: Along with demonstrating our track record in managing change projects, the book highlights an ongoing commitment to sharing insights with clients. As external consultants, we see our role as helping organisations become *change-able*[5] - in what might be termed the 'Emily Dickinson School of Consulting':

---

[5]   Realistically, clients cannot or do not have an appetite to become expert in specialist areas. Key consulting interventions can be delivered 'as needed' in executive coaching, group facilitation, mediation and conflict resolution,

The props assist the house
Until the house is built
And then the props withdraw
And adequate, erect,
The house supports itself
And ceases to recollect
The auger and the carpenter.

Any competent management team can follow the steps outlined in this book. We do not subscribe to the view that all of the 'clever stuff' should be inside a consulting black box, hidden from clients. We guide change processes 'cards face-up', helping management teams to run future change efforts using their own resources. From a business growth perspective, pooling our expertise with clients may seem contradictory. In practice, helping managers become self-sufficient makes great business sense. When it works (and most of the time, it does), we get involved in additional change projects with clients or secure solid recommendations to work with other organisations. In contrast, 'protecting our methodology' is a recipe for low trust, Pyrrhic victories. So, please go ahead and plagiarise the methods detailed. Just do not forget to tell others how you figured it out!

Critical Definitions: To kick-start this journey, let us wrestle with two critical definitions:

- How do organisations work?
- What exactly is organisation change?

Once we have discovered the *answers* to these questions, we will begin to explore how the best-managed companies run change programmes. Buckle in now!

---

management training, employee selection and assessment, etc. The central point is that the client makes the call on this.

THE
TRANSFORMATION
ROADMAP

2

HOW DO ORGANISATIONS WORK?

Your pain is the breaking of the shell that encloses your understanding.
Khalil Gibran, The Prophet

To lead a change project successfully, you need an overall understanding of 'how organisations work'. Just as heart surgeons (healthcare specialists) need to understand the fundamentals of human health, change agents (business specialists) need to know how the component parts of organisations 'fit' together. In simple terms, there are three fundamental tasks that all organisations need to perform:[6]

- Setting direction.
- Staff engagement.
- Strategy execution.

Let us look at each of these in turn.

Task #1: Setting Direction: Executive teams need to be clear about what business they are in/not in and how they intend to compete in that space. They need to decide whether specific 'niche' segments will be targeted. Are they analogous to a *department store* or a *boutique*? And what do customers in these segments actually *want*? They need to

---

[6] There are literally thousands of models that depict how organisations work. In constructing the Transformation Roadmap, the Tandem Consulting team wanted to develop a model that was both comprehensive and yet easy to understand. Perhaps the key point is that a management team needs to work to 'some' model – in order to have a shared understanding of what they are trying to do in a change programme.

decide whether they will compete on price, customer intimacy, or technological leadership – and be familiar with how competitors gain a foothold and defend their space. They also need to determine their level of ambition – whether they want to lead or fast-follow. And so on.

Walt Disney, a clear believer in differentiation, said: "If you want to be successful, look around to see what everyone else is doing, and then do something different". It is technically possible to be successful without a clear strategic direction. In monopoly situations (for example, the ESB for many years) or where markets are growing very quickly (for example, mobile phones), organisations can be 'in the right place at the right time'. Luck does not just apply to individuals. But such cases typically offer relatively short-term advantages. For most management teams, an ability to set clear strategic direction is a critical competency. Over time, organisations that are skilful in this space have a much greater likelihood of success, essentially building the means to 'out-think' the competition. Assessing the clarity of strategic direction is the starting point in determining whether an organisation is maximising its potential. It represents the first 'vital sign' of organisation health. When we are invited to work with an organisation, this 'strategy' question is our first port of call.

Non-Commercial: The *setting direction* issue does not just apply to commercial (for profit) organisations. Many years ago, I did voluntary work in a juvenile offenders' facility in Singapore. While the regime was tough, more than 90% of the inmates were involved in some form of education programme. More recently, I had some contact with Mountjoy Prison in Dublin, trying to provide a bridge for ex-offenders to move into the third-level education system. In contrast, only *circa* 3% of the Irish prisoners were involved in any form of education programme. So, while both institutions looked 'outwardly similar' (high walls, barbed wire, tight security), the mission in Singapore was *educational* and *restorative* while the Irish prison was *custodial* and *punitive*. All organisations need to be crystal clear about their strategic intent and there are wide degrees of choice, even for organisations within the same 'industry' (more on this later).

Future-proof: There is some *genius in the detail* in relation to how both the *today* and the *tomorrow* pictures are fleshed out. While many possible planning approaches exist, the process selected initially should be *divergent* and comprehensive enough to consider a range of possible futures and options. Later, you can *converge* – selecting the key route forward. The most common mistake made in this area is for executive teams to see 'tomorrow' as a simple extrapolation of 'today'. Depending on the industry dynamics, a mix of forces can lead sometimes to a radically different tomorrow. The key strategic questions can be summarised as shown in **Figure 1**.

Figure 1: Future-proofing Your Organisation: Key Strategy Questions[7]

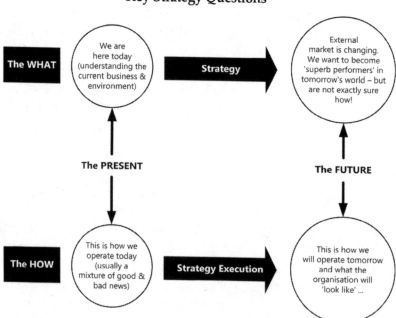

---

[7]   There is no universally-agreed definition of the term 'strategy'. It is used interchangeably to mean: (1) a way to 'think about' the direction for the total organisation; (2) figuring out the best market positions for an organisation's products/services; or (3) a method to 'tease out' the optimum method to move from 'Position A' to 'Position B' (a series of tactical steps). Confused? Welcome to the club! In this section, we are using the term in its widest sense – as a way to consider the direction for the total organisation.

Compelling Truth: The acid test for any Organisation Mission that emerges from this process is that it must be a *compelling truth*. *Compelling* in the sense that it must appeal to the constituencies at which it is aimed (shareholders, customers, community and staff). It also needs to be *true* (or capable of being true at some future point). Basketball nets are set at a height of 10 feet. It is tough to make a basket – but not *impossible*. Organisations should adopt the same logic when setting future goals. They have to be 'tough enough' to provide a stretch target – but not set at a level that people will not even attempt to throw the ball! Practical examples of this are scattered throughout the book in the case studies cited.

Bar Height: Some executives believe that developing a company strategy is about thinking big, 'going for it'. They believe in a managerial proverb that one executive labelled: "The meek shall inherit the shit" and want to set the bar incredibly high. They are like the guy in the James Bond films with the white cat: nothing less than a strategy of total world domination will satisfy their thirst for greatness. In this, they are confusing the concepts of mission and organisation ambition. Sometimes, a consulting dilemma faced is to get organisations to scale back their level of ambition. Let us illustrate with a sporting metaphor.

As I was writing this particular piece, Ireland had been going through the worst patch of weather in recent history. Two bouts of snow, interspersed with endless rain and freezing temperatures. It was not just the banking crisis that connected Ireland and Iceland; we seemed to have imported their weather too! At the same time, golf was being beamed in on the sports channel from Hawaii. The sun was shining there and spectators were wearing multi-coloured shirts. The biggest problem faced by players was rehydration. Blinding sunshine, gentle breezes, dry footwear: what's not to like here? I flirted with the idea of recalibrating my personal ambition. Why not get out of this consulting game altogether and become a professional golfer? Play in good conditions, anywhere hot. Splash on the factor 30 sun block and make a lot of money by turning a favourite pastime into a full-time job. As a strategy, it certainly ticked the *radical* box and was ambitious. There was just one minor inconvenience: a complete lack of golfing talent. Ambition is not a strategy.

A typical strategy workshop design addresses the following objectives (**Figure 2**) and questions. The timelines in **Figure 3** are indicative.

Figure 2: Workshop Objectives

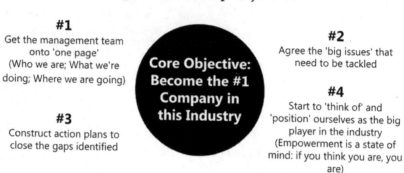

#1
Get the management team onto 'one page'
(Who we are; What we're doing; Where we are going)

Core Objective: Become the #1 Company in this Industry

#2
Agree the 'big issues' that need to be tackled

#3
Construct action plans to close the gaps identified

#4
Start to 'think of' and 'position' ourselves as the big player in the industry (Empowerment is a state of mind: if you think you are, you are)

Suggested groundrules: We are here in a spirit of inquiry: There are no right or wrong questions/answers.

- We are wearing our 'company hat' (not our 'functional hat').
- This is the beginning of a journey, not an end point. We will not resolve every issue in this meeting (if issues emerge that we cannot resolve, we will park these and move on).
- We will run at a fast pace. 90% now is better than 100% never. We stay with the schedule. In practice, we may not have the opportunity to discuss everything in depth.
- Organisational change is a messy process. It does not fall into neat boxes. Sign up for some confusion/frustration in advance.

Question: What additional behaviours would make this meeting a success? (The management team needs to answer this question).

Figure 3: Workshop Flow/Timeline

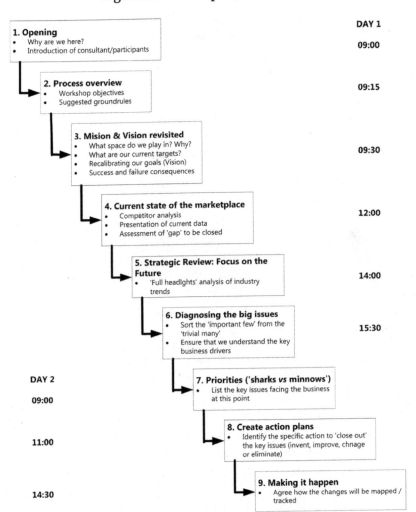

DAY 1

1. Opening
- Why are we here?
- Introduction of consultant/participants

09:00

2. Process overview
- Workshop objectives
- Suggested groundrules

09:15

3. Mision & Vision revisited
- What space do we play in? Why?
- What are our current targets?
- Recalibrating our goals (Vision)
- Success and failure consequences

09:30

4. Current state of the marketplace
- Competitor analysis
- Presentation of current data
- Assessment of 'gap' to be closed

12:00

5. Strategic Review: Focus on the Future
- 'Full headlghts' analysis of industry trends

14:00

6. Diagnosing the big issues
- Sort the 'important few' from the 'trivial many'
- Ensure that we understand the key business drivers

15:30

DAY 2

09:00

7. Priorities ('sharks vs minnows')
- List the key issues facing the business at this point

11:00

8. Create action plans
- Identify the specific action to 'close out' the key issues (invent, improve, chnage or eliminate)

14:30

9. Making it happen
- Agree how the changes will be mapped / tracked

Task #2: Staff Engagement: Once the strategic direction has been set, leaders need to make it emotionally appealing to staff. Strategy creation is not just an intellectual exercise. The best managed organisations figure out how to 'load' the strategy with emotional appeal – crafting something that is powerfully attractive to staff and customers: the challenge of 'a difficult climb', the nobility of a 'socially just mission', the positive pull towards a 'better tomorrow'.

Organisations need to unpack the particular human motivation being appealed to *(pride, success, future wealth, service or survival)*. All of these can work, to greater or lesser degrees of success, within particular organisations and sectors.

Under this heading, some organisations have an easier task than others. Working in a child protection agency is an 'easier sell' internally than marketing a new cigarette brand that targets young adults. Yet the leadership question in *all* organisations is the same: "How do we fully engage internal talent, focusing staff on delivering our strategy?"

Some businesses are more 'people dependent' than others. If you have technologically advanced products or innovative routes to market, the people element in your organisation may not be quite as critical. Yet most organisations, whether manufacturing mattresses or selling internationally-traded services, need to get people turbo-charged. Finding this top-gear is a central leadership challenge as it offers a potential differentiator from your competitors. Engaging the active commitment of staff is the second key organisational dimension that management teams wrestle with.

Task #3: Strategy Execution: Having defined the *promise* (to both customers and staff), the leadership team needs to develop an execution strategy that makes it happen. All too often, we have seen well-conceived strategic plans that are big on *thinking* but small on *implementation*. Sometimes, the management team actually becomes bored with the change journey and abandons it mid-way (avoiding the donkey work described earlier). However, the most common reason for poor implementation is that the management team lacks the project management discipline required to see a change process through to completion. Because results pay the bills, the execution strategy (everything from process re-engineering to sidestepping industrial relations trip-wires) needs to be planned, executed and clinically measured. Strategic planning without execution is empty intellectualism, a form of *managerial dreaming*.

Dual Timeframe: In strategy execution, a key element is to guard against the change agenda being 'under-invested'. The role of all senior executives encompasses a dual timeframe. They must deliver results today, while also building capability for tomorrow. Managing this dual timeframe is one of the most problematic issues for managers working through change programmes – captured best in the seemingly simple question: "Are you working *in* the business or *on* the business?" All too often the day job (working in the business) becomes a black hole and soaks up all the available time.

The magnetic pull of dealing with immediate issues sucks the lifeblood from managers. They then spend their worst hours (at the end of the day or week, often when they are exhausted) in a half-hearted attempt at strategy creation and execution. At best, it is a recipe for mediocrity. This fundamental conundrum of managing today *versus* building tomorrow is overcome in all successful change projects by anticipating this problem in advance and 'structuring' to overcome it (by putting in place the required resources to ensure that sufficient horsepower and time is available to pursue the change agenda). In simple terms, you cannot task an already busy manager with a 'change job' and expect him/her to do both. There is a short-term resource requirement in all successful change projects; organisations that ignore this massively underperform in the change arena.

Vital Signs: Medicine works on the basis that 'health benchmarks' – the perfect readings, as it were – exist. Over time, data is built up from thousands of individual patients and patterns are established. Information on individual patients is compared against this data and a determination made on whether these results are normal or abnormal. The patient may walk from the surgery with a couple of Panadol tablets or be taken by ambulance to the nearest emergency room. It depends on the diagnosis. Our role as Organisation Development consultants works on the same basic principle. Data from a huge variety of organisations is condensed into a composite picture of what a 'perfect' organisation looks like – analogous to the vital signs in medicine.[8] The three key vital signs – challenges faced by all organisations – are setting direction, staff engagement and strategy execution. These have been summarised in the Transformation

---

[8] There are many ways to 'show' the elements in a perfect organisation, along with a range of possible intervention points. This is our attempt to simplify this complex area. It does not matter whether the organisation's managers use an AA roadmap or one produced elsewhere – the key issue is *having a map*.

Roadmap (**Figure 4**), a simple model that is useable by any team of competent executives.

Figure 4: The Transformation Roadmap

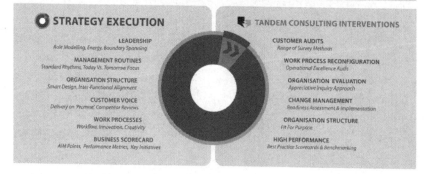

Organisation Roadmap: In managing change programmes, the model is used initially as a 'map' – to aid understanding of how the component parts of an organisation fit together. By detailing the three key 'territories of performance' (direction; engagement; execution), this simplified map allows management teams to understand the building blocks of high performance organisations. It suggests areas that might offer 'productivity breakthroughs'. On the left-hand side of the model, the three key areas are broken out into smaller components. For example, setting direction is sub-divided into mission, strategy and values. The right-hand side of the model outlines practical interventions that can be taken to unleash extra performance under each of the headings.[9] The Transformation Roadmap summarises our view of how organisations work. It provides a shorthand mechanism for us to have a detailed conversation with management teams about which elements of the organisation are working well and which elements need attention.

---

[9]   The areas highlighted are indicative rather than exhaustive. While a wide range of interventions can be made, we wanted to avoid 'presentation clutter'.

3

WHAT EXACTLY IS ORGANISATION CHANGE?

In 1798, Ben Franklin wrote to a friend saying: "In this world there is nothing certain but death and taxes". Samuel Johnson later added that he forgot to mention a third certainty ... change.

In recent years, the world has undergone massive turbulence. Increasing competitive pressures due to globalisation, technology breakthroughs and changing workforce expectations (to name just three factors) have radically altered the arena in which organisations compete. While a small number of organisations somehow manage to thrive on the chaos, most find it difficult to cope with the increasing pace; some find it impossible. The business magazines have extended obituary columns for organisations that, frozen into past practices, fail to meet the challenge and simply disappear from the landscape.[10] Sometimes, the wave is bigger than the swimmer and there is little that local management teams can do to respond. **Example:** In the case of Dell computers in Limerick, the plant closure had much more to do with the delta in international labour costs than any lack of productivity in Ireland. Regardless of the quality of the local management response (and the Dell management team in Limerick

---

[10] The Royal Dutch/Shell oil company conducted a survey on organisational longevity. The result: one-third of the companies listed in the *Fortune 500* in 1970 had disappeared from the listings over the following 13-year period. The average life expectancy for a large company was just 40 years, about half the lifespan of a normal person. The conclusions: only those organisations that have an ability to continually 're-invent' themselves have any realistic hope of surviving in the longer term. The study confirmed what managers understand intuitively: *standing still is a recipe for being left behind.*

were extremely competent), it is impossible to overcome insuperable odds. However, in many cases, it is possible to intervene and help secure the future. In some organisations, changing strategy, employee engagement or work practices (sometimes all of the above) offers a substantial prize, whether this is defined as major market success or simply survival. The central point is that doing nothing is seldom a realistic choice; the target audience for this book is managers[11] who want to do something.

Given the turbulence in the general business environment, it is not an overstatement to say that the ability to implement change has become a core competency. Managing change is now a critically important skill, on par with product, financial or marketing skill. The managerial nous to detect and interpret marketplace shifts and the skills to effect change internally are not simply 'useful traits' to be bolted onto a baseline managerial skillset. The ability to manage change has become a central competence of successful leadership. While there are a range of micro-skills involved in leading organisational change projects, before we drill into the detail let us take a moment to define exactly what we mean by the term change management.

Definitional Issues: As a descriptive term, 'change management' is problematic in the sense that there is no universal definition of what this actually means. Change management is an umbrella term used to describe everything from minor work practice amendments to major organisation overhauls. For example, taking a blood pressure test and undergoing open-heart surgery are both medical procedures – though somewhat different in terms of the scale of intervention. Similarly, the scale of organisation change projects can be enormously varied. A couple of distinctions are worth addressing.

Small *versus* Large: Organisation change projects can be differentiated by size. Projects range from continuous improvement (incremental adjustments to existing methods of working) to quantum leaps (fundamental changes with radically different outcomes). The scale of

---

11   While I am conscious of the distinction, for simplicity the terms 'leader' and 'manager' are used interchangeably throughout the book. A more elaborate exploration of the theme is detailed in Mooney, P. (2009). *Accidental Leadership*, Dublin: The Liffey Press.

the change effort is dependent on the challenges faced by the organisation. The general rule of thumb can be stated as follows: change efforts should be proportional to the size of the challenges faced. Nothing too surprising there. An organisation that is performing well, with no obvious external threat, will tend to make incremental changes. Larger threats solicit a more robust response.

Making smaller (incremental) or larger (transformational) changes is not necessarily an either/or choice. Initiatives under both of these headings can be complementary (see **Figure 5**). However, change programmes tend to follow one or other of these trajectories and the level of 'external threat' should dictate the robustness of internal response. That is the theory. In practice, some organisations would not recognise a marketplace threat if it jumped up and bit them. It is like the old joke about the three types of managers: those who make things happen; those who observe things happening; and those who say "What happened?". As in all walks of life, some people are ahead of the wave while others are reluctant travellers, being dragged along behind the boat, sometimes kicking and screaming that they 'don't want to go there'. Organisational 'greatness' is a moment in time. Major brands can be relegated to second place (for example, Hoover in vacuum cleaners) as their senior teams fail to grasp the nettle of consumer and marketplace changes. In my experience, organisation success sometimes can breed arrogance – with a disbelief that there is a need to do anything to respond. Even where the management team are 'ahead of the curve', it can be difficult to pro-actively communicate the need for this to staff. John F. McDonnell, former CEO of McDonnell Douglas Corporation, stated it as follows:

> *While it is difficult to change a company that is struggling, it is next to impossible to change a company that is showing all the outward signs of success. Without the spur of a crisis or a period of great stress, most organisations — like most people — are incapable of changing the habits and attitudes of a lifetime.*

We return to this key point of communicating the rationale for change later in the book.

**Figure 5: Continuous Improvement *versus*
Transformational Change**

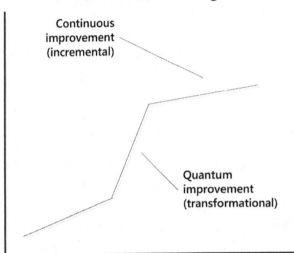

Business as Unusual: Change is an ongoing feature of organisation life, in the sense that all managers 'worth their salt' are continually improving how their particular section or the overall organisation works. But change management, in the sense that the term is used throughout this book, is more than just business-as–usual. It is useful to think of change management as a 'systematic attempt to improve organisation performance with the goal of achieving breakthrough results'. I am not in any way dismissive of attempts to continuously improve organisations on an incremental basis: later on, we will see how a culture of continuous improvement can lead to huge performance gains being achieved over time. But, for the moment, our focus is on breakthrough performance – BIG productivity and performance gains achieved by radically overhauling the way the existing systems work.

Permanent *versus* Temporary Changes: A second useful distinction that can be made is around permanent *versus* temporary changes. Many people who work in the 'change' arena were influenced by the work of an early theorist, Kurt Lewin.[12] The key insight put forward by Lewin was that organisations needed to be 'unfrozen' from their current methods of operation – which corresponds closely with the 'why bother' element of change planning detailed later in this book. Where I differ with the classic Lewin approach is around his idea that organisations subsequently need to be 're-frozen' when the period of change is completed. Essentially, he saw 'change' as an event, a moment in time that needed to be worked through. I see it more as a philosophy, something that needs to be hardwired into the DNA of an organisation. It is not that Lewin was wrong; the rate and speed of changes in the external environment have massively increased since his thesis was developed. The best-managed change programmes guard against a tendency to 'drift backwards'. Even when the BIG change programme is completed – and the layers of organisation fat have been removed – a system of continuous improvement needs to be in place to ensure that the 'weight is kept off'. Lots of organisations 'lose two stone' during focused change programme only to regain the 'weight' (and sometimes more, later).

Not Optional: Given the fluid nature of the external environment, change is seldom an optional extra. Like swimming against the flow in a river, some forward momentum must be made just to stay in the same place. Most organisations have to continuously improve what they do simply to survive the competitive onslaught. It follows that it is useful to think of 'change' as being a permanent, rather than a temporary, state. Managing change is not a moment in time that organisations work through and come out the other end into some new 'steady state'. A brilliant example of 'constant turbulence' is provided in the Lucent Technologies case study (to be found in **Appendix E,** because of its length and complexity). The central point is that the new 'steady state' is continuous flux. An attempt to represent this graphically is detailed in **Figure 6.**

---

[12] For a very useful discussion of this, see Lewin, K. (1947), 'Frontiers of Group Dynamics', *Human Relations*, Vol. 1, pp. 5-41.

Figure 6: The Traditional *versus* the Emerging Model of Change

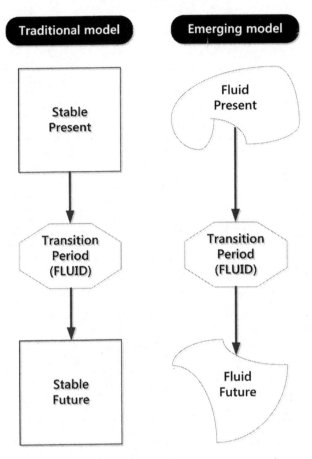

Breakthrough Performance: So, there you have it. Understanding organisations is a precursor to managing change. The Transformation Roadmap provides a model to dissect organisations into three key components. With this model in mind, change management can be broken down into a number of easily digestible stages. By following the steps outlined in the remainder of this book, you will be well on the way to planning and delivering breakthrough performance in your organisation. Let us begin at the beginning by asking a deceptively simple question. How do you plan change?

CHANGE PLANNING: WHY?

4

DEVELOPING THE CORE RATIONALE

Traveller, there is no path, paths are made by walking.
Antonio Machado (1875-1939)

O ur experience in working with companies that have successfully implemented change, highlights three critical questions that need to be addressed during the planning phase (**Figure 7**).

Figure 7: Planning Change: The Three Big Questions

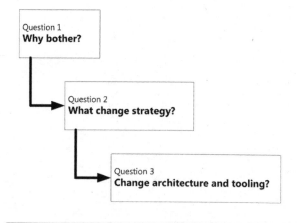

WHY BOTHER?

In considering any organisation change project, the 'why bother' question looms large. Change always involves some *pain* and often a level of *risk*. Typically, some individual (internal executive or an external consultant) facilitates a frank discussion around potentially unpleasant facts: new competition, shrinking margins, decreasing market share, flat earnings, declining revenue or some other relevant metric that highlights a declining competitive position. The purpose of this activity, in the words of a former CEO of a large European multi-national, is "to make the *status quo* seem more dangerous than launching into the unknown".[13]

Key Question: Consider your organisation right now. Is there is enough energy to overcome the normal inertia to drive a change process forward? Is the 'pain' being experienced *today* acute? Is the appetite for *tomorrow* compelling enough to overcome the forces that favour remaining *as is*? Where the 'why bother' question cannot be clearly and forcefully answered, the change process typically will de-rail before it even gets going.

Fire in the Belly: A management team that is 'complacent' about improving performance seldom will have the ambition or the energy required to see a significant change programme through to completion. Some shoot for targets that are too easy. They make the argument: "We are changing" in the same way that people going to the gym once a month claim to be working on their fitness levels. Managing change is a bit like hill-walking. You need to be sure that you can complete the full circuit before you commence the journey – otherwise, you risk being stranded in the wilderness! Better not to start, unless you can make it all the way home.

Concept Selling: At this early stage in the process, the consulting task is to ensure that the senior team are 'sold' on the need for change. If they are not, their energy and ability to convince the workforce of the

---

[13] Kotter, J.P. (1995). 'Leading Change: Why Transformation Efforts Fail', *Harvard Business Review*, March/April. Despite the fact that the article is 16 years old, it can be a useful summary paper to share with the leadership team. It educates and helps to stimulate discussion on change. Worth reviewing.

way forward is severely compromised. The way to *test readiness* is to openly debate the rationale for the change effort, to facilitate internal debates, to allow the naysayers *time in the sun* and ensure that the problems faced and the going forward options have been reviewed from every conceivable angle. This should not be confused with some groups having the power of veto. At some stage, the organisation leader has to call time on the debates and shout "Stop – this is what we are going to do". But internal debates, in which all views are considered legitimate, act like 'mental fitness' training for the management team – getting them ready for an important match before they go out to meet the opposition. In order to facilitate this, it can be useful to introduce an educational component – allowing the management team to explore the normal drivers of change. I often present the following:

- **Change drivers:** Organisation change initiatives are driven by one of two potential motives; they are either *vision-inspired* or *pain-driven*. Let us look at each in turn.

- **Vision-inspired:** The CEO or/and the executive team has a clear picture of a better tomorrow. This is sometimes referred to a 'pull' strategy – a magnetic pull towards an emotionally attractive future. It is worthwhile to try to understand who sits where in this debate. Sometimes, we see strong CEOs push for change against a 'silent' majority of executives and managers. We have often witnessed 'big picture' ideas being pushed forward that have not been thought through or, worse still, a rush towards premature revelation to the workforce. In many cases, we have seen legitimate opposition and alternative views labelled as obstruction and negativity. Key counter-arguments and potential stumbling blocks are ignored as the BIG idea is force-fed through the organisation. But having an idea does not constitute a vision, even if the idea originated in the mind of the CEO. A vision has to represent a 'compelling truth' as defined earlier (compelling = represents a better tomorrow; truth = not so wildly aspirational as to be nonsensical). And, in the *realpolitik* of how most organisations are managed, that vision has to be shared across the management team (better still, by the entire workforce).

- **Shared Vision:** A clearly communicated better tomorrow works by creating dissatisfaction with the *status quo*. This dissatisfaction is a necessary precursor for change and can be likened to the soil preparation stage in planting new shrubs. The organisation needs to be 'readied' for change. Allowing debate around a range of 'alternative tomorrows' is a particularly useful way to move towards this, helping to crystallise the endpoint. Binding people around a common identity is a primary leadership challenge. Kiefer and Stroh[14] hold that organisations capable of inspired performance normally have: "A deep sense of purpose often expressed as a vision of what the organisation stands for or strives to create". What might this look like? **Figure 8** details some of the key questions that describe how an organisation competes in the marketplace. This particular example was developed for Golden Pages (and the company subsequently worked out the answers to the key questions posed).

- **Pain-driven:** While a 'vision of a better tomorrow' can offer a compelling rationale for change, in practice most organisation change projects are fuelled by pain – problems in the existing organisation. The CEO or the senior team ask: "Is the current situation sustainable?" Where the answer is "No", 'push forces' come into play with the organisation being forced to change its *modus operandi*. In my experience, pain is a more normal (and more potent) driver of change than vision. Perhaps it is part of the human condition that we become complacent and are spurred onto the next level of performance only when a 'clear and present danger' enters the horizon. People tend to visit the doctor only when 'there is something wrong'– rather than for a health screening. In similar vein, most leadership teams are energised by underperformance or some threat to the business.

---

[14]   Kiefer, C.F. and Stroh, P. (1984). *A New Paradigm for Developing Organizations*, in Adams, J.D. (ed.). Transforming Work, Alexandria, VA: Miles River Press, quoted in Levy, A. and Merry, U. (1986). *Organizational Transformation: Approaches, Strategies, Theories*, Santa Barbara, CA: Praegar Publishers.

Figure 8: Building for the Future

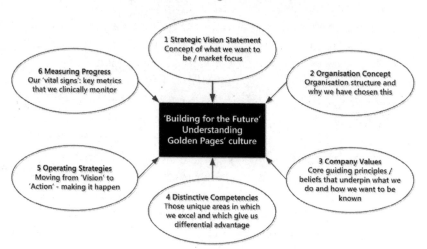

- **Energy Generation:** All change programmes require energy. Management teams can generate high energy is by using the twin drivers of change detailed above:

  o Articulation of the 'pain' (a *push* change strategy).

  o Elaboration of a compelling 'vision' (a *pull* change strategy).

  Push tools align effort through authority and fear ("This is what will happen if we don't change"). Pull tools work through inspiration (a 'better tomorrow') and reward. In practice, the two drivers of change (vision-inspired and pain-driven) are not mutually exclusive but can be welded together to develop a powerful communications message. However, the rationale that drives change tends to have a predominant logic that emphasises one or the other as the primary driver. An outline of how these concepts work is detailed in **Figure 9**.

Figure 9: Push *versus* Pull Change Strategies

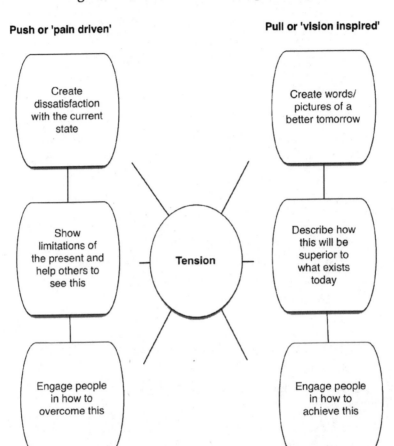

Ok, that's probably enough theory to digest. To bring this alive, let's look at some examples of 'vision-inspired' and 'pain-driven' changes to see how these ideas can be applied in practice.

PAIN-DRIVEN: AN POST

*For many years, John Hynes held the role of CEO in An Post,
the Irish postal service. Historically, the organisation had been
associated with the worst elements of the semi-State sector.*
Example: *To the best of my knowledge, the canteen in the
Sherriff Street sorting office was the only facility in Ireland that
openly sold alcohol to employees who were on duty; there was an
embedded culture of drinking. When the sorting office eventually
moved out to the new Dublin Mail Centre (just off the Naas
Road), which didn't have the same facilities, staff christened the
building 'The Betty Ford Clinic'!*

*In his early years with An Post, John Hynes was seen to be a
positive force for change. He had come through the public sector
system (working previously as the CEO of Bord Gáis) and had
built a strong reputation as a change agent. He clearly pushed a
reform agenda.*

*When John retired, a new CEO, Donal Curtin, took over the
reins in August 2004. Curtin's stint in An Post followed a long
career in the ESB. He installed a revitalised management regime
– which included a plethora of senior team changes. An
immediate shock was the announcement that An Post actually
had been losing money. Losses in that first year were predicted at
circa €20 million – a huge number at that time. The trade unions
in An Post, particularly the Communications Workers Union
(CWU), accused the new CEO of falsifying the numbers –
creating a big stick with which to beat the workforce – using false
accounting practices to leverage change. I was not directly
involved in the An Post change efforts and observed all of this
one step removed – so it is difficult to untangle the truth around
the financials. Were the numbers real or simply a way to 'soften
up' internal resistance? There is no suggestion made or implied
anywhere in this book that financial or other underperformance
issues should be 'invented' by the management team. Quite
apart from any ethical considerations that this poses, within*

organisations there are few secrets; it is almost impossible to gerrymander a situation without this becoming known. The loss of credibility for the management team would be a high price to pay for any supposed gain from creating a 'burning platform'.

Donal Curtin did not have longevity in the role and he left An Post after less than a two-year stint. The central point in the above is that 'announcing' that an organisation is in crisis is not itself a recipe to drive change. One of the key lessons in industrial relations is that threats made have to be real; you cannot fake it. The general consensus is that the most recent CEO, Donal Connell (who chose a completely different entry and subsequent strategy), has been more successful in terms of improving organisational performance.

PAIN-DRIVEN: PRINTCO

One of my own clients is a long established printing company, operating in Dublin. The company has a well-deserved reputation for producing high quality product within a specialist segment of the printing market. The operation was historically profitable and run by a relatively benign management team. The founder, the father of the current managing director, was paternalistic and over time a 'pro-staff' culture developed at the plant. It was a good place to work; in turn, staff produced high quality work. It seemed like a win: win formula.

One outcome of the above was that wage rates rose inexorably year on year – to the point that the company led the marketplace on pay and conditions. By early 2011, printers were earning €1,200 for a 35-hour week. However, strong overseas competition from low-cost printers began to erode margins in the industry. A small number of defections became a flood as customers gravitated towards lower-cost solutions. On several occasions, the MD made the point to the workforce that "There is no sentiment in business" and that something would have to be done. However, the staff in the company simply did not believe the numbers or that the external threat was serious. There had been a couple of 'speed bumps' over the years – but nothing ever came of these. The MD, a brilliant businessman who disliked conflict, was seen to be 'crying wolf'. The workforce had heard it all before and felt they knew how this particular story ended – nothing would happen. This time, they were wrong.

Upping the Ante: *When I became involved in the project it became abundantly clear that the message: 'We have to change or we're in trouble' was not getting through. There was also some inter-union friction in the plant, a distracting issue that clouded the central issue of declining competitiveness. Something had to be done to break through the communications clutter. A summary of the key steps taken was as follows:*

- *The company commissioned the design of a new manufacturing plant in Newry.*

- *It secured planning permission for this, along with grant aid from the Northern Ireland Industrial Development Office.*

- *Management showed the blueprint plans and the supporting documentation to the union officials and the staff in Dublin.*

- *Management pushed for significant changes in both pay and working practices at the Dublin plant – with the overt threat that, if these changes could not be achieved, the entire operation would move to Northern Ireland.*

To reinforce the suggested changes, each employee was given an itemised breakdown of their new net earnings – how their actual take home pay would be affected if they accepted the pay cuts. These numbers were contrasted against what they would receive on unemployment benefits – showing a huge delta between what could be earned by continuing to work (albeit at a lower rate) versus what would come from State unemployment benefits.

Not surprisingly, the staff began to pay serious attention to the threat of job losses, which had become very real. After a series of (difficult) negotiations, it proved possible to reduce wage rates by circa 30%. The pay cuts, along with a number of work practice changes, secured the Dublin plant's viability as competitiveness was restored. An example of the detailed information that was communicated to staff during this major change project is outlined in **Appendix B***.*

Now, I fully understand that not everyone will be 'sold' on the above – seeing it as either an example of managerial bullying or as a sledgehammer used to crack the nut of a simple communications problem. But the net effect was that jobs in Dublin were saved. This 'tough messaging' links back to the earlier points made on making the threat *real*. The role for managers driving change is to paint realistic scenarios of the way the future will take shape — in ways that are *believable* to all interest groups in the organisation.

VISION-INSPIRED: THE NATIONAL COLLEGE OF IRELAND

Commencing operations in 1951 as the Workers' College, over the years rebrandings led to the National College of Ireland. The Jesuit beginnings were evident in the high academic standards, a focus on student support and an underpinning social justice mission in extending educational opportunities into 'non-traditional communities' (usually labelled as 'widening

*participation'). Over time, the college acquired a centre city site
and built a first-class modern facility. However, somewhere
along the way, despite the modern campus, expanded
curriculum and the growth in the student body, the original
focus on social justice and widening participation became
diluted. NCI was operating in a sea of competition, and was a
minnow player versus the six Dublin city-based universities and
Institutes of Technologies.*

*In 2007, I took on the role of College President. After completing
a comprehensive strategic review, it was decided to construct a
new mission statement that, in many ways, took the college back
to its origins with a central focus on student potential:*

**Our mission is to widen participation in higher education
and unlock each student's potential. We offer students the
opportunity to acquire the skills and self-confidence to
change their lives, contribute to a knowledge-based
economy and become responsible, active citizens.**

*To ensure relevance, the mission in all organisations needs to be
challenged periodically. It is as if the air slowly leaks out of the
organisation tyre and needs to be re-inflated. But success is not
determined by the clever 're-wording' of a mission statement.
The ignition of enthusiasm for the new mission is the real driver.
The mission statement is less important than the sense of
mission among the executive team and staff. At NCI, this
nobility of organisation purpose was reinforced at conferring
ceremonies and every other internal communications forum:
"We're not just in the education business. Many colleges can
make that claim. But by offering second chance education and
encouraging non-traditional students to attend third-level, we
are in the business of changing people's lives".[15] The effort here
was to bring the mission 'alive' and to express this powerfully.*

---

[15]   Excerpt from the conferring ceremony speech, November 2009.

> *In essence, we were trying to turn a 'team' of academic and administrative staff into a 'tribe' with a key focus on getting non-traditional students into college.[16] The overall NCI story is complex, with many different elements (not all of them successful). However, my strong sense was that this particular element (getting staff to embrace the new mission) worked particularly well – as it appealed to a higher order motivation – allowing each of us to feel we could make a real difference in students' lives.*

Some examples of 'noble' mission statements (beyond a bland reworking of World-Class and Customer First), are outlined below:

- **Anheuser-Busch**: Someone still cares about quality.
- **Johnson & Johnson**: The Company exists to alleviate pain and disease.
- **Marriott:** Customers are guests; people away from home should feel that they're among friends and really wanted.
- **Merck**: We are in the business of preserving and improving human life. All our actions must be measured by our success in achieving this goal.
- **Nordstrom Department Stores:** A place where service is an act of faith.
- **Sony:** To experience the sheer joy which comes from the advancement, application and innovation of technology that benefits the general public.
- **Southwest Airlines:** Frequency, fares and fun.

---

[16] Some managers find it hard to deal with this 'big picture' stuff. One academic I worked with was described as follows: "She will continue to slice, dice and dissect stuff, mostly commas and full-stops".

- **Wal-Mart:** We exist to provide value to our customers – to make their lives better via lower prices and greater selectivity; all else is secondary.

Overall, remember Sun Tzu's words: "He will win whose army is animated by the same spirit throughout all its ranks".

Burning Platform: Where organisations use 'pain' as the primary lever to drive change programmes, the usual mechanism is to highlight external threats – new competitors, technology improvements and declining financial performance. This needs to be done in a way that captures the imagination of the people in the organisation. Like scenes from a horror movie, the threats need to be made very real. This idea, often referred to as the creation of a 'burning platform', helps to *build legitimacy* for change. The shock of being confronted with negative external market developments or internal underperformance (sometimes both) opens up a sceptical audience to the idea that change is not an 'optional extra'. **Example:** The building society First Active galvanised its people to change after the share price plummeted and one-third of its branch network closed. When Bank of Scotland (Ireland) entered the Irish market, profit margins were squeezed and it became a case of 'do or die'. First Active survived and subsequently thrived, eventually being bought by Ulster Bank in 2004 for €887 million. It is an example of an organising 'using' the moment in time, much as Rahm Emanuel suggested: "Never waste a good crisis".[17] The goal here is to make the 'wolf' more visible, with a threat to survival providing the energy for forward movement. One former Human Resource Director, John McGlynn, used the memorable expression: "You have to back up the hearse and let them smell the flowers".[18]

Let us look at a final example of a powerful expression of vision. This one comes courtesy of Bristol-Myers Squibb (BMS), the pharmaceutical manufacturer based in Swords and Blanchardstown, County Dublin. I worked extensively with the company on this project, which was led

---

[17] Former White House Chief of Staff in the early Obama administration, currently the Mayor of Chicago.

[18] This is a perfect example of McGlynn's brilliant communications skills in action.

by a hard-working and charismatic Chief Executive, John Nason. This is how the company communicated its vision.

VISION-INSPIRED: BRISTOL-MYERS SQUIBB

Future Fit: Our Vision

We will become a pivotal site in BMS, in finished pharma manufacturing and pilot process development. We will lead the organisation in everything we do.

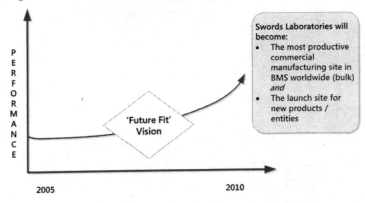

How? By ensuring that we deliver to all of our stakeholders:

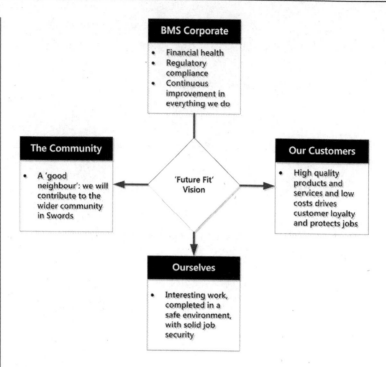

End Goal

A clear vision for our business, giving direction and clarity of focus to everything we do – becoming the most productive site in BMS (Bulk) and the launch site for new products/entities.

A smarter structure, with decision-making power located lower in the hierarchy. We will increase the levels of responsibility for everyone in the operation, engaging the talent we have on-site.

A management team which is fully committed to the new BMS, and competent to take the necessary steps to get us there.

The best customer service record of any unit within BMS world-wide. We will become known for excellent customer relations, fast response time with outstanding attention to detail and follow-through. We will deliver flawlessly.

Routinely go through FDA and other regulatory inspections — as an ongoing part of normal business. No drama.

A system of continuous improvement, change and technology adaptation — leading the way for others to follow. Within BMS the catchphrase will become: "If you want to see excellence, visit Swords".

Creating a Better Tomorrow: What It Will 'Look Like'

Employee roles will contain a number of 'new' elements as detailed below:

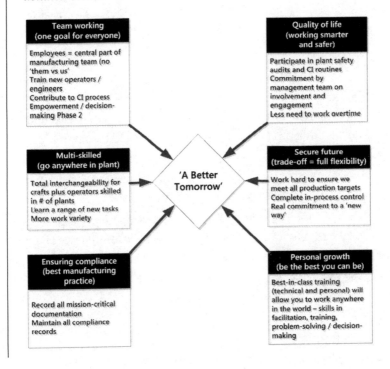

Team working
(one goal for everyone)

Employees = central part of manufacturing team (no 'them vs us'
Train new operators / engineers
Contribute to CI process
Empowerment / decision-making Phase 2

Quality of life
(working smarter and safer)

Participate in plant safety audits and CI routines
Commitment by management team on involvement and engagement
Less need to work overtime

Multi-skilled
(go anywhere in plant)

Total interchangeability for crafts plus operators skilled in # of plants
Learn a range of new tasks
More work variety

Secure future
(trade-off = full flexibility)

Work hard to ensure we meet all production targets
Complete in-process control
Real commitment to a 'new way'

Ensuring compliance
(best manufacturing practice)

Record all mission-critical documentation
Maintain all compliance records

Personal growth
(be the best you can be)

Best-in-class training (technical and personal) will allow you to work anywhere in the world – skills in facilitation, training, problem-solving / decision-making

'A Better Tomorrow'

IS YOUR ORGANISATION 'READY' FOR A SUCCESSFUL CHANGE EFFORT?

This question can be addressed at two levels: first, whether the executive team believes that change is necessary; second, whether this 'readiness for change' is shared across the workforce. We have touched on a staff-level *(pain-driven)* example earlier in the PrintCo case and the efforts that needed to be made to convince the workforce that the threat was serious. Similarly, the attention to detail in the Bristol-Myers Squibb case *(vision-inspired)* demonstrated a seriousness of intent. Let us focus now on assessing executive team readiness. The following checklist of questions is useful in assessing the 'climate for change' within the senior team.

Executive Level: Change will be supported where:

- The organisation is seen to be in crisis – particularly where the 'size' of this can be quantified and is seen to be material.

- The scorecard used to measure organisation performance is more than simply financial. Beyond the numbers, the future capability of the organisation is under threat.

- There is a solid understanding about why the problems occurred and an ability to discuss this – through self-reflection – in a search for solutions not a 'search for the guilty'.

- The executive team has a confident belief in its ability to tackle and overcome the problems faced.

- The executive team has high personal credibility within the organisation.

- There is a sense of urgency – something has to happen NOW to move forward.

Executive Level: Change will be resisted where:

- The executive team believes that the problems faced are temporary, a blip on the radar that will disappear soon.

- The executive team is consumed with the 'day job' – too busy working *in* the business to set aside time for working *on* the business.

- There is an over-concern about maintaining the *status quo* and not upsetting the existing order.

- The problems are seen to reside primarily in specific areas of the organisation – not widespread.

- The Chief Executive is an underperformer or close to retirement.

- There is a downside for individual players (loss of territory/status or short-term bonus payments).

- A poor Chairman leads the Board and there are poor governance routines.

Managerial Scepticism: Not every executive is sold on the benefits of 'change management', partly because of the widespread scepticism around the *science* of this. Sometimes, change efforts fail to live up to their promise potential. Like roman candles, some change efforts are launched with fanfare but quickly fizzle out. Poorly conceived or executed change programmes can lead to frenetic activity and a huge additional workload but produce little forward movement. Lots of heat, but little light. Having 'tried and failed' in this space, some managers believe that change management is the organisation equivalent of snake oil, peddled by unscrupulous consultants selling *hope*. Managers at the coalface, understandably, become sceptical about high cost programmes that do not deliver. It follows sometimes that resistance can be understood as a rational response to poorly conceived plans rather than 'protectionism' or bloody-mindedness on the part of managers.

Do Change Management Programmes Deliver? The central thesis of this book is that change programmes that are managed effectively can deliver productivity breakthroughs. The range of case studies peppered throughout the text underpins this. However, a fundamental conundrum becomes apparent here. Given the general turbulence in the business environment, the need for breakthrough productivity performance has never been greater. Just consider the challenges faced in the Irish public sector at the time of writing. Yet, many organisations are reluctant to embark on organisational change efforts either because of their own or others' past negative experience with the process.

Change programmes are often messy, complex and costly interventions, offering few guarantees of success. Therefore, it is hardly surprising that line managers are sceptical when the term 'change management' comes up for discussion – particularly if it is being pushed by a consulting group (whether the change is successful or unsuccessful, consultants are almost always paid for their time rather than the outcome of the process).

DO STAFF *REALLY* BELIEVE THAT CHANGE IS NECESSARY?

It is not just the management team who are sceptical that change programmes deliver. The same 'hurdle of proof' needs to be overcome with staff, who often do not agree that radical change is necessary.

Staff Level: Change will be supported where:

- The management team has high credibility among the staff.
- A 'clear and present danger' – or an emotionally powerful 'better tomorrow' – is clearly visible.
- Strong communications efforts are made with staff to condition them about the 'new realities'.
- Staff are engaged in designing and implementing the new work systems.

Staff Level: Change will be resisted where:

- The organisation has a history of success over many years – with little experience of having to respond to external threats. In this regard, past successes can actually be a recipe for future failure.
- While there has been talk of increasing competition, real evidence that demonstrates that the market is 'different' may be missing or difficult to grasp. Where the core rationale for change is not easily visible, people will tend to disbelieve or downplay the management case ("Yeah, right! What else would they be saying?").
- Previous efforts to change the organisation have been 'ad hoc' and there was no visible downside (*life has continued as normal*).

- Staff are unionised and the union is difficult to do business with.

- There are concrete losses in the suggested change process (for example, negative impact on terms and conditions of employment).

- There can be change fatigue evident from previous change interventions; people are just 'not up for it'.

WHY ARE THE CHANGES BEING INTRODUCED?

Most organisations managing change are aware of the need to communicate the underpinning rationale – to answer the question "Why do we need to change?". But a mistake often made is that the communication focuses on the managerial logic for change. While staff obviously need to understand the executive team's perspective, of itself this is not enough. Communications need to address the direct impact on employees – captured in the phrase: "Employees listen to WIFM – what's in it for me?".[19] In contrast, organisations that run successful change management initiatives typically go to great lengths to disseminate detailed plans to the workforce – and build employee feedback into the process – making planning and mid-course adjustments. Gaining workforce commitment is seen to outweigh the possible negative of a loss of competitive information (one of the reasons often cited for less effort being made in this regard by some organisations).

You need to ensure that the rationale for the change process is clear and unambiguous and deals with the impact on staff head-on – even where the impact is negative. A variety of communications channels are available to ensure that the central points are understood. But, and this is a key judgement call, you cannot allow the change process to move at the pace of the 'slowest accepter'. Even where external pressures are bearing down on the organisation at the speed of light,

---

[19] I'm not 100% sure of the original source of this great quote. The first time I heard it used was by Michele Keogh, an academic in the National College of Ireland.

such factors are seldom universally recognised. Sometimes, management teams need to plough ahead, despite opposition (see later detailed points on choosing the appropriate change strategy). Waiting until the need for change becomes obvious to all organisational members is a recipe for unemployment! However, all other things being equal, management teams should not commence change projects without making the necessary communications efforts. Great leaders figure out creative ways to drive the 'need to change' message home – as we can see in the next case study.

RESISTING CHANGE: IRISH SUGAR

Irish Sugar had two manufacturing sites: one in Carlow and the other in Mallow, County Cork. The company was established in the early days of independence of the new Irish state, as part of the country's efforts to become self-sufficient in food production. A key element in this was providing a stable income to the farming community. The price paid to farmers for the raw material (sugar beet) was reliable, with annual negotiations pushing the price slowly upwards. From a productivity perspective, Irish Sugar was riddled with poor practices. These were obscured from view by dint of the fact that it held a monopoly position – no other company supplied sugar to the Irish market. Over time, the attractiveness of the Irish market became apparent to competitor organisations which, when deregulation came into force, flooded the market with cheaper sugar products. It became clear to the management team that something would have to change – to guard against further loss of market share.

New Manager: *Joe Walsh, a young manager, joined after a long stint in engineering within General Electric. I had worked directly with Joe in GE for a couple of years and had come to* *admire him as one of the best people managers I'd ever seen in action. A fitter by trade, he brought a 'shop-floor' perspective to his dealings with people and was hugely engaging. If General Electric was Manchester United, the work practices in Irish Sugar were the equivalent of a Saturday afternoon kick-about. Walsh recognised the chasm between the current company performance and where they needed to be. However, a combination of weak management and strong unions meant that the organisation was paralysed. Threatened strike action, over many years, had led to a position where the unions held the upper hand within the company, with the engineering shop stewards holding a key power-broker position. Walsh understood that, in order to get movement, he would have to get this group on board. As a former tradesman, he had a good personal link with the group – but not strong enough to persuade them to relinquish their power position acquired over many years. I was working alongside Joe in a consulting role during this time and we discussed a range of options to 'make the wolf visible'. Eventually, we came up with the following idea.*

Blind Tasting: *People within the sugar industry prided themselves on 'product knowledge'.[20] The management team had been pushing the message internally that low-cost imports were threatening the dominant market position. The staff understood the point but effectively were in denial – arguing that consumers were able to differentiate between 'low-quality, cheap imports' and 'high-quality Irish Sugar'. To overcome this resistance, we set up a blind tasting test whereby the shop stewards of the various unions had to 'taste' the difference between sugars from various locations (Northern Ireland, Caribbean, etc.). It was a high-risk strategy. If they could successfully differentiate the*

---

20   I had seen the same phenomenon in an earlier project, while working with a cheese manufacturer in Kilmeaden, County Waterford. At the heart of this reaction was a pride in being able to manufacture a unique food product – something that could not be replicated anywhere else. But that pride is only justified if the consumer shares this view.

sugars, the management team's arguments would evaporate like sugar in boiling water (literally); so we said a couple of 'Hail Mary's' in advance of the experiment. During the test, the shop stewards could not tell the difference between the Irish and the imported sugar – which was selling at a huge discount. This critical intervention became the turning point in a major change programme that was launched at that time to help the organisation restore its competitiveness. While the company subsequently closed down (Irish Sugar could not compete based on manufacturing costs alone), arguably the intervention led by Joe Walsh extended the life of the organisation by several additional years.

What's in a name? Some organisations like to 'brand' change programmes to help differentiate them from normal work. Here is a selection of names that I have used in the past:

- Enterprise One.
- 2020 Vision.
- Mission Possible.
- Scramble for Profit.
- Future-proof.
- Game-changer.
- Horizon 2010.
- Merlin.
- Chapter 2.
- Catalyst.
- Turning Point.
- Strategic Framework.
- Reach.
- Performa.

- Quest.
- Amarách.
- Airborne.
- Breakthrough.

The key is to select a name that has some internal meaning in the organisation. Overall, it is normally helpful to be able to refer to the change programme in shorthand (provided that the 'name' does not create cynicism internally).

Change Appetite: Creating a baseline appetite for change is a vital first step in the management of change. This is done by asking and answering the 'why bother' question. Without this *fuel in the tank,* the risk is that a change programme will launch but quickly fizzle out. Like a lot of the ideas, it is simple – but not simplistic – that is, it works in the real world. Let us move on now to the second big question at the planning stage – what change management strategy should you adopt?

5

CHOOSING A CHANGE MANAGEMENT STRATEGY

The problem with the future is that it usually arrives before we are ready for it. **Arnold H. Glasgow**

S electing a change strategy that will work for your particular organisation is the next step in the planning phase. The central question that needs to be addressed under this heading is "What change management strategy will we adopt?". A couple of separate (and very different) options are potentially available. Management teams need to understand and consider each of these before locking on to a specific change strategy.

Custom Fit: Often, change programmes are presented as if they were recipes, a specific series of actions carried out in a particular way to produce the results desired. Consulting organisations sometimes collude with this *one best way* idea, particularly firms that market a specific A, B, C-type change model. In reality, there are usually several choices. Consider for a moment the process if you were building a house. You would (rightly) expect the architect to find out a little about your family and how you live rather than simply giving you an 'off-the-shelf' generic structural design. Would you prefer a music room, a garage or a gym? Do you need space for visitors? A home office? Similarly, in deciding the specific 'method' to deploy in change management, it is critical to understand the organisation culture, the challenges faced, the future plans and the quality of the executive team.

In broad terms, change strategies range along a continuum from 'sell' to 'tell'. You choose a strategy that fits with the current organisation needs and future requirements. Organisations are as individual as people. The key lesson: don't be 'sold' a particular approach unless if it is custom fit to your circumstances.

Buy In: An element of 'political correctness' often enters the senior team's debates at this point. Participative methods (sell) are seen as the *only* acceptable means of engaging staff in a change process. The term 'buy-in' has become part of the standard managerial vocabulary, to the extent that many people believe it is a prerequisite to effective change. It is not. In practice, change programmes have opportunities for alternative courses of action and the organisation should consider a 'range of options' before deciding the best route forward. While this is more art than science, I have found the following model useful in choosing the optimum route.

TYPOLOGY OF CHANGE STRATEGIES

The level of organisation change (continuous improvement *versus* radical transformation) and the mode of change (the extent of involvement of the workforce) will differ between organisations depending on the challenges faced. In broad terms, this leads to two choice options:

- **Type A:** *Participative* **Change:** Sometimes, change is achieved through collaboration. This is normally used when an organisation needs *adjustment* but time is available and key interest groups broadly favour change. It is used also in circumstances where very strong interest groups (for example, hospital consultants or university academics) can veto change by the 'management' team. Participation in change has been a cornerstone of the Irish public sector change process – for example, consensus underpins the Croke Park Agreement.

- **Type B:** *Forced* **Change:** Sometimes, change is achieved coercively, often where the necessary conditions for participative change are not in place. Forced change is used typically when time is short, key interest groups continue to oppose change (for example, at the end of an extended negotiations period) or radical change is vital to organisational survival.

The approach chosen (A or B) will depend on the circumstances within each organisation and the volatility of the external environment. Let us use an extreme example to make the point.

Pilot's Decision: Let us assume that you are a passenger on a commercial flight from Lisbon to Dublin and a technical problem with the aircraft emerged during the flight. Would the pilot conduct a quick passenger survey to see what they think should be done? Perhaps have a vote on an alternative airport to land at, one that would be least inconvenient? Is it not important to get 'buy in' from passengers who could be future customers of the airline? The suggestion seems somewhat absurd. In these circumstances, we expect top-down decision-making – using the criterion of 'safety first'. There is no democracy at 36,000 feet, nor is any expected. In similar vein, an organisation facing a 'clear and present danger' may also need strong (sometimes, unilateral) leadership to avoid closure.[21] The Chief Executive role is similar to the role of a pilot in this regard. Both are responsible for the continued 'safety' of the organisation and this should dominate their thinking.

In contrast, in an organisation not under immediate threat engaging staff around the co-creation of a better future is often the best way forward. If there were a Ladybird book explaining psychology, the first lesson on page one would state: "People don't resist their own ideas". But staff engagement is not just using psychology to overcome resistance. People are potential oil-gushers of creativity and the role of the leadership team is to unleash this potential.

The broad argument can be summarised as follows. Engaging the workforce *usually* makes sense in terms of allowing people to put their fingerprints on the change process and become active participants in this. But this method is not always available. Depending on the criticality of the circumstances faced, a top-down or 'forced' change strategy may be entirely appropriate. Too often, we see examples

---

[21]   There is a view that powerful leadership has its own 'change impact' on an organisation. Most readers will be familiar with the George Bernard Shaw line (*Man and Superman, 1903*) that: "The reasonable man adapts himself to the world; the unreasonable one persists in trying to adapt the world to himself. Therefore, all progress depends on the unreasonable man".

where management teams confuse 'means' (process) with 'ends' (results). You need to stay neutral on the means – selecting the method that will deliver the best result for the organisation. Why? Because results pay the bills! Resistance to change is not always the result of poor communications or some other misdemeanour on behalf of the management team. Sometimes, it is an active attempt to derail the process – based on conflicting interests. Let us take a look at an example where there was massive resistance to change and try to understand the dilemma faced by the new CEO who took over the reins.

TEAM AER LINGUS: RESISTING CHANGE

While the mid-1990s seems like ancient history now, the points that emerged in this specific case are still completely relevant. Way back then, I had an opportunity to work with TEAM Aer Lingus, the aircraft maintenance company. The operation was located at Dublin Airport. Most people who have flown from Dublin have driven past the massive gray hangers located across from the old terminal building. The company completed all of the maintenance work on Aer Lingus aircraft and also worked for a number of international airlines on a contract basis. The general consensus within the industry was that the quality of maintenance work completed at TEAM was first-class. While the facility was relatively new, the workforce typically had long service – having moved across from the main airline when Aer Lingus outsourced its maintenance work.

So far, all good news. The bad news was that, at an organisation level, the company was massively underperforming. Terms and conditions of employment were at the high end of the international spectrum while productivity and efficiencies dragged along the bottom. One manager described it as a 'culture of expectancy' – in relation to pay and working conditions. The fact that most of the staff had been employed in a semi-State organisation (and held the infamous letters of comfort guaranteeing them a return to the main airline) made it an extremely difficult place to manage. The company had just come through a disruptive strike – in which the airport roundabout was picketed, which severely disrupted the functioning of the airport. My role was to work with the senior team (of 70+ managers) and develop new ways of working.[22] The situation was not sustainable; something had to be done;

I was conducting a range of one-on-one interviews and running focus groups to better understand the organisation. During one of the interviews, one of the maintenance engineers summarised the predominant culture as follows: "It's all go around here, isn't it?". I hadn't been overwhelmed by the pace of work and kicked to touch: "In what sense?". "Well, it's go to the shop, go to the credit union, go to the travel department. Go fucking anywhere, except go to work".

Elephant in the Room: *Undoubtedly, there were a range of positive elements in the TEAM Aer Lingus operation (the quality of the personnel and the clinical safety record were both outstanding). But a huge overreliance on overtime working was a cancer in the organisation. Overtime working rewards negative behaviour, as tasks that should be completed during normal hours are done outside of this. Labour hours normally paid at flat time (the hourly rate) are paid at time +50% or time +100%, depending on the schedule. In TEAM Aer Lingus, when people worked on bank holidays they were paid two days' pay plus a day off in lieu (effectively 300% of basic). These premium rates were paid on top of what were already high basic earnings, pushing labour costs into the stratosphere. The negative effect of this was compounded by the second factor noted above – low*

---

[22] For a more detailed discussion of this project, see Mooney, P. (1999). *The Effective Consultant*, Dublin: Oak Tree Press.

productivity. The combined impact was that the company eventually became uncompetitive.

Where wage rates become out-of-step with the market, the problem is normally incremental. It creeps up on you until, one day – BOOM! The organisation becomes out of sync with its competitors. Contract Managers within mainstream airlines, the people responsible for working with aircraft maintenance partners, flew their planes to Germany and Korea to have the maintenance work completed (this is the ultimate mobile market). And those jobs in TEAM Aer Lingus – along with the fantastic engineering tradition that underpinned them – left the country, probably forever.

In good times, many organisations ignore the scourge of overtime working – particularly in industries where labour costs are not seen as *material*. The effect is that an alternative work system becomes ingrained in which slowing down, rather than speeding up, is rewarded. A full discussion on overtime working practices is outside of the scope of this book. However, the central point is that 'resistance to change' is not something that can simply be overcome by better communications or clever employee engagement. It is not that staff do not *understand* the rationale for change. Sometimes, they understand it all too well – but have a different *frame of reference*. In change programmes where attempts are made to dismantle existing working arrangements, resistance is not an aberration – it is a natural and expected part of the process. While much of the academic material on change management suggests that 'engaging the staff' is the magic bullet to overcoming resistance, the question: *Qui bono?* (Who benefits?) needs to be addressed. Not all change programmes are positive; in practice, the *better tomorrow* picture may not apply equally to all stakeholders. In these circumstances, a *forced change* strategy may be 100% appropriate.

Confident Stance: The early stages of change programmes typically are ambiguous and often confusing. In my experience, this level of ambiguity is almost always anxiety-provoking and stressful. Senior executives, somewhat more attuned to living in a 'grey' (not black and white) world, can cope better with this. When junior staff are involved, people who have not been exposed to this level of uncertainty, they can become stressed or even form a view that the senior team 'don't have a clue what they are up to'. So efforts to engage staff in the very early stages of creating a new strategy, although well meaning, sometimes can be counterproductive. Successful change programmes need to be led with confidence. Assuming that you have not graduated from the 'crystal ball school of management', you will not have all the answers. So how can you be personally confident when you do not have the answers mapped out? The way to overcome this is for the executive team to communicate short-term certainty. I often advise executive teams to 'be confused in private, but confident in public'. In the world of change management, honesty (in the sense of being totally open about the inner feelings within the senior team) is not always the best policy.

In a recent interview, General Norman Schwarzkopf was asked if he thought there was room for forgiveness toward the people who harboured and abetted the terrorists who perpetrated the 9/11 attacks on America. His answer was classic Schwarzkopf. The General said, "I believe that forgiving them is God's function ... OUR job is to arrange the meeting". People in organisations expect the senior team to lead with confidence – once this does not spill over into arrogance. I am reminded of a conversation with one client, who asked: "Have you read Bertie Ahern's autobiography?" "Eh no, not yet. Is it good?" "Well, I'm on page 187 and he hasn't put a foot wrong yet!"

SETTING REALISTIC TIMEFRAMES

Q: How long does it take to change a large organisation?

A: Longer than you think!

There are no exact time guidelines in this space – as it very much depends on what exactly you are trying to change. But there is some *science* underpinning this. Blanchard and Hersey[23] detail four *levels of change:* knowledge; attitudinal; individual behaviour; and group or organisational performance changes.

A hierarchy of difficulty is experienced in effecting change when moving through each level. The relative levels of difficulty and time relationships are set out in **Figure 10** below.

Figure 10: Managing Change: Time Span and Level of Difficulty

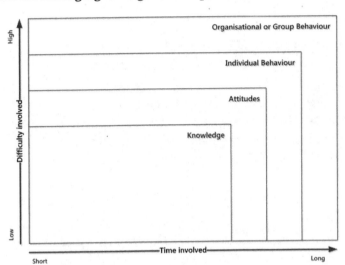

While it may seem paradoxical, sometimes our role is to advise management teams to slow down. Large-scale organisation change projects need to be run like a marathon. Management teams can put huge effort into the planning and the early construction phase but burn out prior to execution. They run the first part of the race at a 100-metre sprint pace – and their energy declines as the project moves into the implementation phase.

23   Blanchard, K. and Hersey P. (1972). 'The Life Cycle Theory of Leadership', *Training and Development Journal*, Vol.23, No.5, pp.26-34.

6

CHOOSING A CHANGE ARCHITECTURE

The final question under the 'change planning' heading is: "What framework (change architecture) will we use to guide the programme?". We have already made the point that successful change management programmes are tailor fit to the individual organisation – 'off-the-peg' options are not as effective. However, you do not have to start with a completely blank page. Invention is great – but plagiarism is quicker and cheaper – and you can draw on materials developed by others. There are a couple of particularly useful frameworks available under this heading – and we consider three specific examples.

Project Planning: At the heart of all change management programmes is a list of key actions that must be delivered. Construction projects provide a useful analogy and executive teams can learn from the methods used in that sector. The goal here is to use project-planning disciplines to ensure each element of the change process is progressed. The concept is hardly revolutionary; this is equivalent to a construction blueprint, a method used by the ancient Egyptians in building the Pyramids (*usefulness* rather than *newness* of ideas is always a more interesting question). A modern day version of this helps to keep the diverse elements of a change programme on track.

Multi-Faceted: Managing a large-scale organisation change is typically multi-faceted. Several 'tracks' (changing strategy, organisation structure, staff engagement, up-skilling the management team, redesigning reward systems, re-designing key processes, etc.) need to be managed side-by-side. Successful change efforts require attention being paid to each individual element. Construction projects require a foundation, walls, a roof and internal plumbing; all the 'bits' are needed. Someone (typically the site foreman) has a plan with a defined end point and systematically follows through on this. "Is the wiring finished?", "Why are we delayed on the window installations?" and so on. Likewise in organisation change projects, the individual elements form part of an overall jigsaw – with each element receiving management attention.

Change Room: If the change is large enough and will take some time, it can be very useful to dedicate a 'Change Room' (sometimes referred to as the 'War Room') — a physically separate structure – from which all of this work is completed. In addition to providing physical space for the change team, it often has an indirect benefit of sending a signal of 'seriousness' throughout the organisation. Sending a powerful 'we mean business' message can help to overcome any lingering scepticism about the organisation's intent to follow through. Communications is not just about the spoken word – but critically also about *messaging* – demonstrating the new behaviour required through role modelling and staging 'events' that underscore the organisation's intent.

PROJECT ARCHITECTURE: STRUCTURES USED TO GUIDE THE CHANGE PROCESS

Under this heading, we will consider three separate change management structural options. The first two (Strategic Framework and Transition Planning) essentially are top-down planning systems. The third (Workout) is a bottom-up implementation method.[24]

Option A: The Strategic Framework[25]

The 'strategic framework' is a change management planning and implementation process. It allows organisations to systematically

---

[24] For ease of communication, the options are presented separately. In reality, they could run side-by-side. For example, the 'top down' nature of the Strategic Framework could sit easily side-by-side with the 'bottom up' Workout strategy.

[25] I first came across this framework working with Mike Davidson, a brilliant USA-based consultant, who worked with Cap Gemini. While the exact origins of the model are unclear, my understanding is that it was developed several years earlier in Andersen Consulting.

'think through' how the organisation will compete going forward and to track progress against this. The process of constructing a strategic framework is detailed below:

- **Step One:** A group of senior managers define the mission, values and measures of success for the organisation.

- **Step Two:** They debate the 'critical success factors' in the business. The core question is: "What do we need to do brilliantly in order to be successful in the marketplace in which we compete?".

- **Step Three:** Key strategies/goals are developed that will deliver against each of the critical success factors. These provide the 'targets' that will be used to measure progress. The critical success factors tend to be relatively stable. The key strategies/goals are shorter-term focused.

- **Step Four:** The senior team develops specific action plans to make each goal happen. This moves the concept beyond 'visioning'; this is essentially the planning stage in executing the vision.

- **Step Five:** For very large organisations (multi-product, multi-country), the process is repeated at appropriate levels in the organisation. The first two elements (mission and critical success factors) typically remain fixed across the organisation. Local units then 'fill in the blanks' for their operation.

The strategic framework is completed initially with the line business units. The format can be used subsequently to 'align' staff groups (Finance, HR, Marketing). The bottom line is that enormously complex businesses, with a diverse portfolio of products and activities and working across multiple geographies, can use a centralised planning method to ensure they stay in lockstep.[26] Specifying centralised elements (mission, values, etc.) alongside local planning (goals and

---

[26] Some organisations do not encourage centralised planning in this way. A well-publicised international example is J&J, which is known for the local autonomy granted to subsidiaries, which essentially operate as independent companies. In Ireland, CRH probably provides the best example of this 'de-centralised' value (albeit this is changing somewhat).

implementation steps) – allows an organisation to 'think global, act local'. The strategic framework can be used for 'normal business planning' – it is not specially designed for organisations undergoing periods of change – but it can certainly be used for that purpose. An outline of this comprehensive framework is detailed below.[27]

STERLING WINTHROP

Our Mission

We are a worldwide team committed to creating distinctive solutions for the needs of mankind in pharmaceutical and consumer health products. We measure our success by the achievement of market leadership, superior financial returns and an environment of trust and personal growth. We accomplish this through the dedication of all of us and all of our resources to continuous improvement in all that we do.

---

[27] To avoid any 'insider trading', I have used an example from some years ago. Sterling Winthrop was a $2 billion pharmaceutical company, which sold a range of over-the-counter, and prescription medicines. Panadol and Solpadene were the best-known OTC products in Ireland, with Bayer Aspirin being the best-known product in the USA. The company was bought during one of the many consolidations of the industry and is now part of GlaxoSmithKline. There was much more detail in the original construction, which was produced as an A3 page; the example shown communicates the key elements and has been simplified here to communicate the basic concept.

Measures of Success

Customers	Employees	Shareholders
Market position – 75% of brands over five years on the market in the top three positions.	**Trust –** 90% of employees rating company performance to be satisfactory or better on questions related to trust in employee survey.	**Sales Growth** – Grow new sales 3% points faster than the market.
Reputation (for service) – 90% of markets/countries ranked in top quartile as determined by customer service survey	**Personal Growth** – 90% of employees rating personal growth opportunities to be satisfactory or better on questions related to personal growth in employee survey.	**Profitability** – Operating profit among the top three world-wide competitors.

Our Values[28]

We are a winning team: We believe that we will succeed only as a team and that the full participation of all is essential to the fulfilment of our mission. It is imperative that we create an environment of mutual respect, candor and trust; where all can reach their highest potential; where individual initiative and performance are recognized and rewarded; where all identify with the success of the company; and where a winning attitude prevails.

We are customer-driven: We believe that the success of our business depends in understanding and satisfying the needs of the consumer. Market needs must drive our choice of products and services and the way we deliver them. At the same time, success in delivering those products and services requires that the recipients of internal services and staff work deserve the same consideration so that all our activities create value.

---

[28] A full discussion on the question of Organisation Values is outside of the scope of this book. I have covered this topic in some detail in an earlier publication: Mooney, P. (1996). *Developing the High Performance Organisation*, Dublin: Oak Tree Press.

We are dedicated to continuous improvement: We believe that sustained success depends on the maintenance of superior quality, which we only achieve through continuous improvement in everything we do. In a dynamic, competitive world to stand still is to be left behind. We encourage a healthy dissatisfaction with the status quo and the creativity and initiative to do something about it. Openness to change, to experimentation and to the search for a better way characterises our attitude to every aspect of our work.

We have a sense of urgency: We believe that being first, speed of action, hard work and an aggressive determination to get things done are characteristics of every winning team. In our business they are a condition for survival. The first to market has an often insurmountable advantage. The quickest to move keeps everyone else off balance. The will to succeed very often wins the day through sheer determination.

We act responsibly: We believe that integrity is an essential asset. Our success is worth having, and ultimately will occur if our every action is characterised by staying true to our values, and the best of each of the societies in which we live and work. We will always do the right thing.

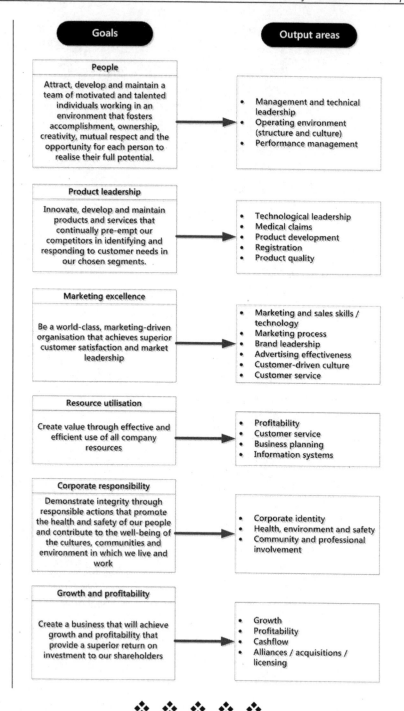

Transition Planning

The Transition Planning model (**Figure 11**) contrasts a diagnosis of the current situation *(today we are...)* against a going forward vision *(tomorrow we will be...)*.

Figure 11: The Transition Planning Model

Today we are ...	Change Agenda	Tomorrow will be ...
Our customers ...		Our customers ...
Our processes ...		Our processes ...
Our direction ...		Our direction ...
Our profitability ...		Our profitability ...
Our growth ...		Our growth ...
Our technology ...		Our technology ...
Our products ...		Our products ...
Our values ...		Our values ...
Our leadership ...		Our leadership ...
Our culture ...		Our culture ...
Our measurements ...		Our measurements ...

The 'change agenda' items emerge from the question: "What do we need to do to move from today to tomorrow?". These 'today *versus* tomorrow' questions can be posed against a number of organisational sub-elements (customers, processes, etc) that are customised for the individual organisation.

In this way, a 'map' of the organisation – how it looks today *versus* how it will look tomorrow – is clearly drawn. The beauty of this model is the *simplicity* in developing and communicating what needs to happen to change the organisation.

The Workout Model

In order to involve people at 'lower' levels, some organisations develop a formal engagement mechanism. Probably the best-known example is the 'Workout' model used extensively in General Electric.[29] When Jack Welsh was the CEO of GE, he was nicknamed 'Nuclear Jack' on the basis that he 'killed the people' but left the buildings standing.[30] During the time I worked with GE, Welsh's efforts to delayer the organisation resulted in a workforce reduction from 400,000 to 260,000 employees. The Workout Model was developed during that period and was based on the simple notion: "Now that we have taken the people out, we need to take the *work out* of the organisation". A war was launched internally against all non-value-added activity.

Bottom-Up Implementation: GE developed a system to train all staff in the removal of non-productive activity, under the overall label 'Workout'. While not, of itself, a brand new idea (industrial engineering had been around since the 1920s), what was unique about the GE experiment was the systematic way it was implemented across the entire organisation.

Workout Principle: The Workout Programme was built on a number of underlying principles:

- Empowerment starts with candour and trust. Performance data should be shared with the workforce (hardly revolutionary now, but a big leap at that time).

---

[29] The exact origins of the Workout Model are unclear. The company had 'experimented' with earlier versions of this – for example, I was responsible for researching Quality Circles in a GE manufacturing plant in Dublin many years before the Workout Programme was formally launched. GE was known to 'swim close' to the academic community in the US, ensuring that leading edge thinking about organisations was incorporated into how the company operated. These senior academics also taught at the GE 'university', in Crotonville, upstate New York. Somewhere, in all of this mix, the Workout Programme was born. There is no debate around the fact that the 'engineering culture' within GE was a good fit with the 'tools' in the Workout Programme. This, coupled with the centralised culture (GE was quite *military* at that time in terms of centralised policy-making), meant that the programme was systematically rolled out across almost 300,000 people, in what some staff described as the biggest 're-education' programme since the Chinese revolution!

[30] This was a fallout from the GE strategy at that time. GE wanted to be (or become) the number 1 or number 2 company in any business sector it competed in. If this was not possible, it exited the business resulting in the closure of a number of plants and the subsequent reduction in the workforce.

- Treat staff as the experts they are; no one knows more about a process than the people who are working on it everyday.

- While change has to be driven from the top, it has to be implemented bottom-up; this approach engages the entire workforce, regardless of job grade.

- Use process tools/discipline. The implementation of Workout requires a re-skilling of the workforce – giving them access to engineering skills and process disciplines more typically associated with 'graduate level' positions.

- In the Workout programme, employees have the power to make real changes. In return, they are expected to take on more responsibility. It is both permission and obligation.

- A high % of recommendations do not cost much to deliver.

- While not every employee-led suggestion leads to breakthrough performance, small steps add up to large gains.

WORKOUT SESSIONS: HOW IT WORKS[31]

Task 1: *Process Improvement.*

Method: *Group spends time (about 15 minutes) 'brainstorming' how to improve some aspect of their work routine – for example, customer service.*

Task 2: *Indicate degree of impact[32] and difficulty of change[33] – by placing each item in the 'Service Improvement Matrix' (in GE, this matrix became christened the 'CRAP Detector').*

---

[31] This is a very stripped-down/simplified process flow. It may be *too* simple. If you wanted to use this technique, there is an argument for developing more comprehensive materials in a 'Service Improvement workbook' — and make this available to all employees.

[32] Will this reduce a lot of work, unnecessary expenditure, speed-up the process, help our customers, reduce inventory etc?

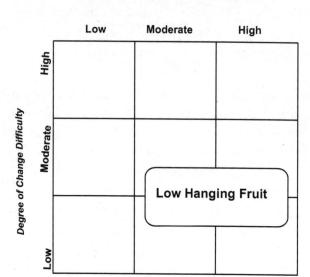

Task 3: *Determine who needs to be involved to change this (assign a letter to each work elimination item): Me Alone = M; Our work group = G; Intergroup (ours and another) = I; Total organisation = T.*

Task 4: *Create an action plan for the 'low hanging fruit' items that can be changed quickly and which have impact.* **Question:** *What's the most broken? (what needs fixing first). Involve relevant parties.*

Task 5: *Get ready to present these issues to your line management team.*

Sign-Off Meeting: *The purpose is to make quick decisions on process simplification ideas generated by the workforce. A subsidiary goal is to provide a 'quality check' to ensure that necessary/vital process steps are not eliminated.*

Method: *Local line managers meet with each team. At this meeting, the team presents its analysis using the 'CRAP Detector' format. The local managers 'sign-off' using the 'traffic*

---

[33] How 'embedded' is this item? How difficult will it be to change this?

lights' system, where green means 'Go ahead', amber means 'Possible but ... needs more study (specify)' and red means 'Stop: don't do it!.

Task 6: *The implementation of the agreed items is project-managed. Responsibility for following through stays with the local team. A follow-up meeting/process is determined (specific dates, etc.) with the line managers to ensure that agreed items are actioned.*

The key steps in the Service Improvement Programme are:

Change (What)	How Measured?	Actions Required	By When?	Owner

An Evolutionary Process of Change: Some of the earlier approaches to change could be described as 'revolutionary' – they are BIG BANG changes, radical overhauls of existing systems. They are the organisational equivalent of the TV programme, *Extreme Makeover*, where a house gets knocked down and is completely rebuilt. In contrast, the Workout programme is typically a series of small evolutionary steps. In this sense, it is more in keeping with what we earlier defined as continuous, rather than quantum, improvement (see **Figure 5**). However, and this is a critical point, the systematic implementation of the Workout programme (or any similar programme) leads to the development of a culturally very different organisation in which the opinions of staff are sought and acted upon. So, while the individual change initiatives may seem 'small beer', cumulatively there can be enormous gains over time. The internal marketing of this within GE was labelled as 'Finding a Better Way, Everyday'. The effects (during my time there) were as follows:

- **Process Impact:** Removal of non-value-added work by slimming down bloated processes ("If we were starting this factory again, how would we redesign the processes?"). Elimination of 'boundaries' between work areas; processes typically 'cut-across' work areas and have zero respect for the existing organisation structure. **Focus = Increased Speed.**

- **Behavioural Impact:** Workout gets more people into the *change game*, eliminating the traditional blue collar/white collar divide. Decision-making is moved to the lowest possible level in the organisation with a heavy increase in training and development – particularly focused on shop-floor staff. A positive by-product is an increase in trust and mutual respect as the workforce and the management begin to define problems in a mutually inclusive way. **Focus = Staff Empowerment.**

Before Work-Out[34]	After Work-Out
"We don't trust the company; they don't trust us" "Our opinions don't matter" "We're treated like a pair of hands" "Staff are blamed for all quality problems" "We don't know how the pieces fit together"	"Trust is building" "Our opinions matter" "We're treated with respect" "Most quality problems are resolved at the process level – not by individuals" "We are starting to learn how the whole system works"

The Ohio 'Skunk Works' Visit: I remember making a trip to Ohio during the time when I worked for General Electric. This enormous plant (there were traffic lights in the staff car park) manufactured 'white goods' – a range of washing machines, fridges and freezers. In typical GE style, the facility was run along military lines. Crisp, clean

---

[34] Internal GE communications material. The goal was to explain the process to managers and solicit their support.

production, brilliant housekeeping, smart dress code among the management team (short hair, white or blue shirt, always a tie).

In one corner of the facility, there was a smaller unit where the *creatives* worked (that was how this group was labelled). The unit was full of competitor products in various states of disassembly. GE bought competitor equipment and the engineers took them apart to see how they worked. The goal was to improve the design and build quality of GE's own equipment. It was striking that the engineers in this part of the facility looked 'physically different'. Casually dressed in jeans and t-shirts. More ponytails on display than at the Dublin Horse Show. It seemed somehow 'anti-establishment' (these sub-cultures were later to be memorably labelled as 'skunk works').[35] This divided site, a mainstream manufacturing plant run with precision side-by-side with a smaller 'innovation reservation', represented the underlying philosophy at that time. 'Workers' (blue-collar manufacturing personnel) performed in well-managed, tightly-controlled production units; their job was to 'do'. The 'staff' (white-collar engineers) were tasked with process improvement; their job was to 'think'. The Workout process was revolutionary in the sense that it turned-on-its-head the notion that only 'staff' could contribute to process improvement. Every employee was now seen to be part of a *continuous improvement* system. There were no 'separate' parts of a factory that were tasked with being 'creative'; every part of the operation had to continually improve. Just consider the numbers. Approximately 1% of staff in the Ohio facility was involved in the 'skunk works'. Extrapolating a similar percentage across the entire company would provide 2,800 people directly engaged in continuous improvement. In contrast, the Workout programme envisaged all 280,000 becoming involved in this area. While it is unlikely that GE ever achieved 100% in this exercise, you can see from the above the potential power of this philosophy being put into practice.

You Are Here! At this point, you have a solid understanding of the overall change process. You have also considered the three key steps in the planning phase. The early components have now been assembled.

---

[35] The name was first mooted in Peters, T. and Waterman, R. (1982). *In Search of Excellence,* New York: Warner Books.

You know why your organisation needs to undergo a change programme and broadly how you are going to approach this. What is required at this point is to select the change *targets* – the specific issues that you are going to improve. One thing that becomes crystal clear in managing change is that *you can't upend everything at the same time.* The senior team needs to focus on a couple of central targets – the shark issues. We now turn our spotlight onto this phase in the change journey.

CHANGE
TARGETING: WHAT?

7

CHOOSING KEY CHANGE LEVERS

If you have always done it that way, it is probably wrong.
Charles Kettering

N ow that you have a comprehensive understanding of the change process – the attention shifts to this *selection* phase. Choosing specific change **targets** moves to the top of your 'to do' list.

Choosing Targets: Imagine for a moment you were driving along the road and, unexpectedly, your car broke down. You check the petrol gauge. Nothing wrong there: the car had been filled up during the week. You then get out of the car and open the bonnet to see if anything is obviously amiss. A passerby, seeing you in obvious distress, helpfully suggests: "Have a look at the wiper blades. They look quite worn to me".

I am pretty sure that you would ignore this advice. Even if the wiper blades were 100 years old, they are unlikely to be the source of the breakdown. In similar vein, when management teams review organisations, there are a myriad of potential change targets. Some of these will be *central* and some will be *peripheral* in terms of their impact on organisation performance. The critical management task at this juncture is to select the levers that have potential to offer a performance breakthrough. The Transformation Roadmap detailed earlier can help you to identify the most likely areas to focus on (strategy, people, operations). Before we look at this in more detail, there are a couple of contextual points. Buckle in for a tiny bit of theory.

Unique Organisations: Every organisation is unique – in terms of history, culture, products and people. In identifying change targets, there is no foolproof guide. Change targets cannot be pre-ordained; they must be selected on a case-by-case basis. **Lesson:** Change targets selected need to be shaped around the challenges faced in your particular organisation.

Holistic View: Many change management models emphasise a *formulistic* approach (strategy, process re-design, re-organisation, customer service improvements, then staff engagement, etc.). Sometimes, consulting companies that have a particular expertise drive this idea that change needs to be managed in a very precise sequence. In one outrageous example of 'selling in', a UK-based firm of organisation psychologists that operated in Dublin for many years invariably diagnosed organisation problems as stemming from poor 'chemistry' within the executive team. The *solution* (which they just happened to have in their briefcase) was an 'Executive Development Workshop', which would supposedly right all the ills of the organisation. Many executive teams struggle to get everyone on the same page – so there was always some purchase in the suggestion that all is not well in Camelot. But, even if the executive group can be turned into a team of champions, this does not guarantee the success of the overall organisation.

Assuming that the diagnosis is crystal clear, a *single-issue* approach to organisational improvement can make sense. But you need to be really careful that the change targets selected are the true performance drivers – and not just the result of a management or consulting team bias. For example, if a group of friends go to a restaurant, some might be particularly interested in the quality of the food, others in the friendliness of the staff, while some might remark on the cleanliness of the toilets. All three views about the restaurant are legitimate – but the 'fixes' (assuming that any element was not working) are very different. If you are focusing on a 'single issue', just make sure that you have the correct target in your sights!

NEW COMPETITORS: TELECOMS INC.

Tandem Consulting recently worked with a telecoms company that decided to embark on a new strategic direction. The old product line, while profitable, had become generic and somewhat jaded; all its competitors were offering essentially the same stuff. But some new entrants had 'changed the dynamic' – beginning to compete (and make real market inroads), focusing on relationship management rather than price. The offer to customers was 'end-to-end solutions' – making buyers' lives easy – instead of simply selling hardware (which the customers actually installed). You can see the attraction. When you have a puncture, do you want to purchase a new tyre for your car and fix it yourself? Or would you prefer to drop the car into a service station, grab a cappuccino and a newspaper and pick up the car when the old tyre has been replaced? The new competitors had moved aggressively into the full-service space and Telecoms Inc. had to move fast to catch up.

The company set up a series of internal project teams to better understand these trends. There were a number of integrated elements to this research (customer feedback, competitor product testing, envisioning the future, etc.). When each strand of the project had been completed, the material was synthesised by the senior team and a new strategy for the company began to emerge from what had previously been a fog of confusion. The company then moved into an implementation phase to ensure that this 'better tomorrow' actually could be delivered. We facilitated robust conversations about the 'today' organisation (what was working well; what was broken) and how practices would have to change to deliver the new strategy. All of this was led by a powerful CEO. He was genuinely fearful that, if the company did not change, it faced extinction. He often used the line: "Sacred cows make the best burgers", and used this philosophy to overhaul the existing organisation radically.

> *It is still too early to state definitively that the revised strategy has been a success, but the early signs in terms of customer feedback and financials are both trending in the right direction. The customer defection rate has been staunched. And the company has been clever at understanding the new competitor offerings and building its own offering on top of this (sometimes, being a 'fast follower' has many advantages; it is not always about being first to market).*

Diagnostic Success: The success of such projects is dependent on the diagnostic phase being completed correctly. In the example given, the competitor moves were reasonably simple to ascertain and a counter-strategy was built. However, at the diagnostic phase, unravelling external market changes or internal organisation performance is seldom clear-cut. During this phase, it makes sense to take a holistic view of the organisation before locking onto a specific 'change agenda'. In essence, you need to give yourself permission to remain confused for a bit longer while you make sense of the data. When *speed is the only criterion used, you just get to the wrong place faster!*

Central Point: Management teams need to use a variety of approaches to interrogate performance rather than over-relying on a single view of the world. Targeted approaches to change are OK, provided that you are 100% certain that the crosshairs are focused on the key organisation issues. The message here is very simple. Take time. Consider the problem from a range of perspectives. Try to be aware of your bias (the management or the consulting team if you are using external support). Make sure that the diagnosis can explain all the variables. And do all of this before you lock-on to the specific change agenda. Why? Because no amount of 'executive teambuilding' will fix a product or marketing problem. And likewise, a brilliant marketing strategy will not overcome the presence of a toxic CEO. It's easy, right?

Psychological Dissonance: The above recommendation seems easy. In practice, it is difficult to get senior teams to 'stay in the fog' long enough to ensure that they really understand the problems faced, often because of what psychologists label *dissonance*. It works as follows. When a person holds two contradictory views, this creates dissonance – an anxiety that makes them feel uncomfortable. The simplest way to overcome this is to move from 'two views' ("I might go to America on holidays *or* I might go to Australia") to one view ("I like Australia best"). This principle comes into play heavily in organisation change projects. Typically, it pushes executives towards a 'single diagnostic point' too soon in the process. Locking onto a single solution ("Let's fire Mick O'Neill and that whole group will be reinvigorated") provides a strong sense of movement ("It's about time we tackled that guy"). That's the good news. The bad news is that you would be better off working on the right issue. Otherwise, you can end up making a raft of changes, but the original presenting issues will resurface. You need to get comfortable managing in this ambiguous space. F. Scott Fitzgerald (*The Great Gatsby*) suggested that: "The test of a first rate intelligence is the ability to hold two opposing ideas in mind and still have the ability to function".

False Cause and Effect: At the time of writing this particular section, there is a public debate in Ireland about the dress code for parliamentarians. A group of recently-elected politicians had 'dressed down' – attending parliament without wearing jackets or ties. This led to a pushback from some of the more traditional members of the Oireachtas. In defence of their 'informal dress code', some of the newly elected members argued that the bankers and financiers whose reckless lending behaviour and high bonus culture led to the fall of the Celtic Tiger often were impeccably dressed. Therefore, being 'well dressed' was no guarantee of good performance. The argument in favour of an informal dress code was cleverly framed as follows: "Which would you rather have? A conservatively-dressed politician, or an honest politician?". In this instance, two completely different issues become confused. The real question is: "What is the appropriate dress code for an elected member of Government while on duty?". But this argument becomes entangled with the general antagonism against senior bankers for poor lending practices. It is a clever piece of obfuscation – but completely irrelevant. In organisation change projects, a similar dynamic can take place. The job of the consulting team here (who, by definition, should have more objectivity) – is to 'disallow' false cause and effect analysis. **Reminder**: Does the 'solution' chosen answer all of the presenting issues in the organisation?

Skills Blend: In order to complete a holistic diagnosis, organisation executives need to have a blend of skills – they have to be more than 'one-trick-ponies'. If they have been recruited from a predominant discipline, for example accountancy, they will tend to 'see the world' through that particular lens. But, at the diagnostic phase, you have to actively guard against 'locking on' too soon to familiar solutions. It follows that some change programmes are doomed from the start – through incorrect initial diagnosis. Like the motorist in the earlier story, some management teams do a great job changing the wiper blades, but the car still will not start! So, how do you decide what to *lock onto*?

SELECTING TARGETS: FOCUS ON THE VITAL SIGNS

Picture the scene. When a patient walks into a GP's surgery, the doctor performs a series of diagnostic checks – usually fairly quickly. From this examination, he or she can produce a scientific health evaluation. The speed and accuracy of the assessment is possible because of a clear understanding of *what is important*; doctors know what to look for based on the four *vital signs* of human health:

- Body temperature.
- Pulse rate.
- Blood pressure.
- Respiratory rate.

From these simple measures, the doctor can make a reasonably accurate diagnosis or determine whether further investigations are needed. It is not foolproof. We have all heard stories about when the diagnosis phase went horribly wrong – but, thankfully, it works well most of the time. While management consulting cannot claim the same longevity as medicine, there are many similarities. In the business world, consultants play the role of 'Company Doctor', tasked with helping to determine *organisational health*. The client's assumption is that the consultants can help them to diagnose strengths along with underperforming areas that need attention – and do this quickly and cost-effectively. The key challenge for any consulting team is to develop an organisation diagnostic model, the equivalent of the vital signs in medicine – a model that allows a reasonably quick (but accurate) assessment of organisation performance. The Transformation Roadmap provides this holistic 'lens', ensuring that the change agenda is not overly influenced by a particular functional bias.

Complex Organisations: Any useful diagnostic model needs to meet three key design criteria. First, it must be comprehensive in order to be usable across a range of different organisations (public sector, commercial, not-for-profit, etc.). Second, as we have argued earlier, the approach needs to be holistic. Some approaches focus exclusively on 'hard' elements – for example, organisation structures or processes, not least because these are the easiest elements to measure. Alternative approaches are based on expertise in the so-called 'soft' organisation elements – for example, customer attitudes, vision, engagement and culture. Successful change projects pay attention to both *hard* and *soft* organisation elements and any model needs to emphasise both elements.[36]

Organisation Alignment: The Transformation Roadmap model focuses on the totality of organisation endeavour. **Central point:** In our consulting work, we have come across a number of change management initiatives that did not produce lasting change. In trying to unravel this, several times we encountered design elements within organisations that were actually *contradictory*. **Example:** You cannot change the reward system, without impacting the culture and *vice versa*. In the same way that food intake and human energy levels are not two *separate* things, the Transformation Roadmap demonstrates how the various organisation components are *connected*. It is like the

---

[36] One CEO remarked: "In trying to change organisations, the 'hard' stuff is easy and the 'soft' stuff is hard". Willie Slattery, CEO, State Street Bank, presentation in the IFSC, March 2011.

words of the old song: "The knee bone is connected to the thigh bone...".

Customised Approach: Any model needs to be capable of being customised to the needs of individual clients. **Example:** Performance management systems have a very different *shape* in the not-for-profit sector, where a focus on staff *development* is often as important as the *performance* element. While there are a number of generic elements in all successful organisations, effective change initiatives are custom-built to fit specific organisation requirements. You cannot take a change programme designed for AIB, remove the logo from the cover page, and pretend that this has been designed for Bank of Ireland. It simply will not work. Of course, there will be common elements (this entire book is prefaced on the idea that common elements exist in all change programmes), but this should not be confused with a 'cut and paste' suggestion.

Targeted Changes: One final point is worth making. Not every organisation needs to start at Point A and work its way to Point Z of an organisation change roadmap. In the airline industry, there are four 'levels' of maintenance. After each flight, the aircraft has a routine, *in situ* physical inspection – known as an on-line or 'A' check. The checks become progressively more elaborate, up to and including a major overhaul – known as a 'D' check. Not every organisation change project needs to be a D check. Sometimes, it is a major overhaul; other times, it is just new spark plugs! The central role for a consulting group is to facilitate clients in exploring how the overall organisation works and to understand performance in each key area. Once this baseline understanding is in place, executive teams then *choose* individual components to overhaul.

Cracking the Code: Organisations, at times, can seem hopelessly confusing. Products, processes, people, markets, distribution channels, stakeholders and a host of other elements combine to create a fog of confusion. The Transformation Roadmap combines the individual elements into a 'picture', showing how each of these interacts. Using this map to guide their thinking, management teams often can choose instinctively where to focus attention, 'zooming' into those areas with most performance improvement potential. After reviewing the roadmap, we normally work alongside management teams on a number of simple (but important) questions as follows:

- What is the current 'mission' for this organisation? What is the central promise made to customers and staff? How clear is this (both to them and to us)?

- How well are we performing against this mission? How do we know? What objective criteria do we have to measure our current performance? Are these financial or broader measures?

- What are our key strengths as an organisation? What unique capabilities do we have? Why do customers like doing business with us?

- Do we have data from customers who do not work with us or who have left us? Do we understand this 'external viewpoint'?

- Where are we currently feeling the most pain and why? What are the big issues that continually emerge? What keeps us awake at night?

- Which areas represent the biggest opportunity to improve our performance? In relation to the current operation, where is our worst underperformance? Is this in an area of strategic importance?

- Where is the market headed? Are there emerging trends (threats or opportunities) that we need to be mindful of? How do we know?

- What are the issues, internal or external, that are blocking our progress? Are these 'hard' or 'soft' issues or some combination of both? How can we overcome them?

- Assuming that we were successful in tackling the central issues identified, would this allow us to fundamentally improve our competitiveness?

- Is there any dynamic in our own senior team that stops us pursuing this agenda – even if this is awkward to discuss?

- Is there any dynamic in our organisation culture that blocks us from becoming the best in this business?

Deep Dive: Gaining a deep understanding of an organisation is a complex task and goes well beyond developing a simple list of presenting issues. A comprehensive diagnosis should unveil a hierarchy of issues and the 'cultural norms' that act as an invisible hand steering day-to-day behaviours. The medium-term goal is to ensure that all of the elements in the organisation are aligned and facing in the same direction. In practice, in order to get this deep understanding of the organisation, it is usually necessary to take sample views from various levels in the hierarchy to build a representative picture. The view from the *bridge* is seldom the same as the view from the *engine room,* captured in the phrase: "Where you sit is where you stand!". Sometimes, we get pushback from management teams when we suggest a comprehensive data-gathering process. They see it as long-winded – analysis paralysis – when they just want to "get on with the job". Our role, paradoxically, sometimes can be to slow-down executive teams at the front-end of change programmes. The core argument is that conducting in-depth diagnostics does not mean that the overall timeline is elongated. Well-planned change programmes (slower front-end) can be executed quickly and effectively.[37]

Understanding Culture: A key question that often emerges is: "Can you change an organisation's culture?". The short answer is: "Yes, you can". The longer answer is: "But, it is not easy to do".

In several transition programmes, we have been asked to help 'change the culture'. Organisation culture can be described in shorthand as 'the way things are done around here'.[38] It is an umbrella term, combining both 'hard' (systems, policies, procedures, rules) and 'soft' (beliefs, shared values, organisation history) elements. One way to view organisation culture is as a combination of the things that, taken together, form the *personality* of an organisation – but it can be a difficult concept to grasp. One executive I coached expressed his

---

[37] A full discussion of this is outside of the scope of this book. For a more detailed explanation, see Mooney, P. (1999). *The Effective Consultant,* Dublin: Oak Tree Press.

[38] Deal, T.E. and Kennedy, A.A. (1982). *Corporate Cultures: The Rites and Rituals of Corporate Life,* Harmondsworth: Penguin Books.

frustration with the concept as follows: "I would love to meet this guy, culture. He seems to be blocking everything round here".

Strong, pervasive cultures turn organisations into cohesive tribes with distinctly clannish feelings. The language used reinforces the values and traditions of the tribe. Catchphrases, tales of past heroes and behaviour in day-to-day operations (for example, how customers are treated when they come to the counter) – combine into a rich collection of ideas and actions that form the organisation culture. Culture is also enshrined in rituals (for example, for new starters, for leavers, for promotional events). The culture also can be identified in the 'artefacts' that the organisation uses (the shoe-cleaning equipment that was in place at one stage in Bank of Ireland's staff toilets is a good example of this). Just as some individuals have particularly strong *personalities*, some organisations also have a distinct style. New employees tend to adapt to these practices fairly quickly (technically, they become *acculturated*) and may be *corrected* if they violate the organisation's norms. Or they leave.

Culture can be explicit or implicit: some organisations want to make their culture explicit — known, understood and *implemented* by all employees (for example, Intel's Six Values, which are heavily publicised internally). In other organisations, while there is no written statement of culture, it can be implied from policies and procedures and, most potently, from observing management behaviour. The central point is that culture influences performance. That is why organisations are interested in exploring this topic. The arguments in favour of having an explicit/strong company culture are as follows:

- **Goal alignment:** The organisation wants to get all of the troops marching in the same direction. People only support what they understand. Having a crystal clear set of goalposts is the best way to achieve this. Making the organisation values clear (for example, customer service or speed) provides 'behavioural goalposts' for employees to follow.

- **Motivation:** The organisation wants to communicate to staff that they 'stand for something' to ensure that the full motivational impact is unleashed. Making elements of the culture explicit (for example, medicine before money in a private hospital) helps to source that discretionary effort.

- **Low bureaucracy:** Shared values guide behaviour without the need for stifling bureaucracy and control systems. Some organisations want employees to automatically 'make the right calls'. Having a clearly articulated set of values guides them in this.

- **Avoiding slideback:** I first heard the term 'culture eats strategy for lunch' in Bahrain while working with the Royal College of Surgeons in Ireland (RCSI) on a new hospital project. RCSI's then-CEO, John Horgan (since retired) used the phrase to describe how the culture in RCSI was supportive of overseas expansion. Where a culture is strong, it often provides an 'invisible force'. Better to understand and 'work with this' than to ignore it or swim against the tide. **Example:** In the third-level sector, the concept of 'academic freedom' is very strong. There are many examples of 'university strategies' that did not work simply because this underlying 'cultural' element was ignored and effectively put a block on changes that the senior teams in universities tried to implement.[39]

In working with organisations to explore their culture, the following checklist of questions can be helpful:

- What are the five or so 'key beliefs' that people in this organisation share? What words or phrases best describe these?

- How were you made aware of these (written format, stories, part of a formal induction, celebrations, creation of heroes, etc)?

- How do these underlying values/beliefs shape the way that employees behave on a day-to-day basis?

- What 'evidence' do you have for the above? (old stories you have heard; actual examples you experienced or witnessed).

---

[39] A full discussion on this is outside of the scope of this book. However, some of it is simply 'resistance' masquerading as a principle. Academic freedom is often another name for 'freedom from management', worth another book in itself!

- What 'works well' in the existing culture? For example, how much has the culture valued customers? How widely shared is this?

- How much has the culture valued employees? How would you describe this?

- Has the culture valued stockholders/financial performance? What is the evidence for this?

- What elements of the culture have changed over the past 10 years and why? Have some long-standing traditions been abandoned?

- Overall, do you think that the existing culture has helped or hurt the performance of the organisation over the past number of years?

- What do you see as the negative elements in the existing culture and would like to change?

Change Agenda: Let us assume for a moment you have an executive team that is 'ready' for change – in the sense of being open to reviewing how the organisation has performed to date and aware of the need to create a 'better tomorrow'. By systematically working your way through the steps detailed and reviewing the three core elements in the Transformation Roadmap, a menu of change management targets will begin to emerge. To establish a *new* culture, executive teams have to give considerable thought to developing organisation rituals, celebrating when progress is made towards the new outcomes (thereby reinforcing the new culture). Or they may have to consider moving away from current beliefs. Sometimes, these ideas can seem counter-intuitive. For example, if you heard that an organisation had decided to 'get rid of some customers', you might be surprised. But that is exactly what the Electronics Payments Company decided to do – and it made perfect strategic sense.

ELECTRONIC PAYMENTS INC.

This client company experienced a steep decline in market share. While there was lots of anecdotal evidence around individual customer defections, it was difficult to pinpoint the exact causes or to make sense of the trend in a turbulent (but growing) marketplace. The only objective evidence was the rate of client 'burn' – running at circa 20% per annum. We were asked by the company to stop this revenue haemorrhage.

Approach: The first port of call was to understand the organisation history. As part of this, we took an in-depth look at the relationship with customers, running focus groups with key 'buyers' and speaking with external influencers within the sector. We also shadowed a couple of 'reps' on visits to customer sites to witness the front-line relationship at first hand. Finally, we engaged key staff in drilling down into specific customer defections – both the causes and potential ways to resolve it in the future. The promise to staff was 'no search for the guilty'; just an exploration of solutions. Once they were assured that 'no-one would get into trouble', they proved remarkably open, explaining exactly what was happening.

The outcome of this project was the customer segmentation 'framework' detailed below. A key finding was that customers were not a homogeneous group. In reality, there were highly profitable and highly unprofitable customers – with some occupying the in-between space. This conclusion led to the question: "Should we offer the same service to all our customers or do we have Gold, Silver and Bronze standards?" A final categorisation of customers emerged as follows:

A CUSTOMERS
"Mind Them"
- high-level service contracts

B CUSTOMERS
"Charge Them"
- charge for terminals

C CUSTOMERS
"Sack Them"
- move them to a competitor

Building Tomorrow: Using the framework detailed, we captured the going-forward strategy for the business as follows:

Key Goals: We need to...	We will Know We are Getting There When...
Strategy #1 Capture and retain great customers ...	High revenue/turnover from each customer Our customers are loyal to us Credit-worthy Low maintenance Recommend us to others
Strategy #2 by offering a great product	Reliable ('works the same every time' — consistent) High performance (Breakdown = >99.5% uptime) Ahead of competition (innovation/new products) Fast (<10 seconds) User-friendly product (our machine = customers' 'product of choice')
Strategy #3 In an 'envelope' of great service ...	Superior to competition; every point of contact works well Consistent quality from everyone User-friendly (each process = clear/simple) Positive interactions/friendly Our service level is measurable Proactive (not waiting for problems to be highlighted) Bottom line: we are easy to do business with
Strategy #4 helping to 'create tomorrow'	Creating 'space' (crystal-ball forums, spending time on *tomorrow*). We plan 'ahead of time' Bolt on additional opportunities with 'ease' — NPI process = smooth/easy for customers See products through customers' eyes (not *technical*) Innovative: we have an internal capability to 'think outside the box' (or buy this externally)

A range of specific change initiatives was developed and professionally closed out by the company. Tandem Consulting worked alongside the senior team as each stage of this project unfolded.

Project Result: 100% retention of 'A' customers, including the re-recruitment of a number of defectors, and 88% retention of the 'B' customers. In practice, the efforts to move away from 'C' customers proved the most problematical part of the strategy and was less successful. The project highlighted a key lesson in change management, which I have seen repeated time after time. The 'hard lifting' is investing sufficient effort into completing the diagnosis phase systematically. When the executive team has a deep understanding about what is happening now and what they want to happen, figuring out 'what to do about it' often is relatively simple.

Clear Roadmap: It is sometimes helpful for a management team to understand how the overall change programme will work. While this can be clear in the mind of the consultants, it does not automatically follow that internal managers 'get it'. I have found it useful to highlight the various stages that a change programme goes through and to make these visual/graphic to aid understanding. An example of this was the Irish Rail project on customer services (see below). We used this 'Three -Phase' Roadmap to keep the project 'on track'.

IRISH RAIL: CUSTOMER SERVICES IMPROVEMENT PROJECT

Anyone who has travelled by train in the past five years will know that Irish Rail has invested heavily in rolling stock and rail tracks (continuous weld tracks help to overcome the traditional 'clickety clack' of train journeys). Result: the physical level of service improved substantially. I became involved in a project that was focused on the personal service given by Irish Rail staff. Goal: ensuring that all face-to-face transactions with the customers matched the investments in track and infrastructure.

Improving Service: Considerable effort had already been made to determine customer feedback (mystery shopping reports, etc.). This indicated that there was significant scope to improve the customer experience, moving it onto a programmed, systematic footing. This type of programme is not just about changing staff attitudes — but also the systems that underpin how service is delivered. Many of the people in Irish Rail consider themselves to be part of an engineering tradition — working for a transport organisation, rather than a service company. There was no clear customer service value identified in a universal way by the staff. We defined the purpose of the project as follows and built a three-phase change process to make this happen:

- *Support the executive team in creating a Service Vision.*

- *Ensure that roles and responsibilities are crystal clear in relation to driving a Service Culture.*

- *Enable the middle management team to manage staff — reinforcing service behaviours at all levels of the organisation.*

- *Inspire the staff to embrace a service culture/teach service behaviours and engage with them in making the transitions needed.*

- *Develop a common service language that will become part of Irish Rail culture — that people can access and use on an ongoing basis.*

Phase 1: Research & Diagnosis: "What are the key customer service issues today?"

Key Questions/Steps

- *What is in scope/what is not (for example, investment in infrastructure — moving from single to double track on the Kildare line).*

- *Data gathering is not simply a 'technical' exercise, but the start of a political/change process. How do we involve the various stakeholders here – the senior team, middle managers, the trade unions? We need to manage this project smartly –*

we don't want to be de-railed at a later point. How we announce the project and who we meet are important decisions here.

- *We need to 'tap into' what already exists in terms of customer feedback (existing data). We also will conduct a thorough review of complaints – to understand service failures. We will then have a view on how the 'voice of the customer' can be accessed on an ongoing basis.*

- *Every organisation has '100 things wrong' — our job is to come up with a hierarchy of issues that would really make a difference ("What do customers really value?"). Need to sort 'sharks' from minnows.*

- *We could work with an internal team (or several) to 'sort through' the issues and develop a hierarchy vis-à-vis "what the customer wants/expects from us".*

- *Review/evaluate the current training activity (Training Centre Inchicore) – to determine the 'today' picture.*

- *Mapping where the critical 'moments of truth' occur. An examination of all key transactions with customers (and the tangible and intangible services that flow from this).*

- *Consultants personally need to spend time as 'observant customers' and gather 'benchmark' data/charters from other large organisations.*

Senior Team 'Hot Buttons'

A number of important issues have already been highlighted…

- *Lack of consistency re customer experience ("It's hotchpotch").*
- *Punctuality ("We need to run on time – no excuses").*
- *Poor signage: Hard to know 'where we are'.*
- *Can we identify/anticipate 'repeat offenders' – for example, Autumn leaves on track/Sandite machine availability for the high profile lines.*

- *Car parking spaces to ensure we are 'good neighbours'.*

- *Ensuring maintenance is conducted against a 'customer service priority list' – for example, keep the Dart and Dublin/Cork trains running on time.*

- *One company vision: Everyone in the company (from cleaners to engineers) needs to have a customer service vision that they can relate to.*

Outcome: *At the end of this phase, we will meet the senior team to present our initial findings.*

Phase 2: Build a Customer Service Vision: *"We need to work to build a fantastic customer service plan – with short-term fixes and long-term vision"*

Key Questions/Steps

Why Bother? *We need to 'build the business case' – showing the reasons why customer service is critically important. This needs to dovetail with the current five-year plan and support the case for additional future investment. Subsidiary questions include:*

- *Who 'owns' customer service? We need to give each of the target groups (executives, line managers and front-line staff) ownership of this concept.*

- *How can we make this initiative serious/memorable? Part of the answer = slogans and internal merchandising. More of the answer = real engagement and defined expectations for each 'level'.*

- *Need to understand what is expected from the various 'layers' in the organisation (leadership team, middle managers, support groups and front-line staff).*

- *One 'simple' methodology is to build a "Today we are ..." plan versus a "Tomorrow we will be ..." plan.*

- *We need to build a storehouse of language around brilliant customer service – and choose a metaphor that reflects the process underway (for example, house renovation, an epic journey, etc.).*

- *Empowerment: What is the scope for employees' decisions?*

- *When we 'build the plan', we need employees to challenge this, to push back and to add on elements. This part of the process needs to be led by the senior team. We need to be aware of the cynicism/push back, which will come from some managers and staff.*

- *Staff Training: A number of short/sharp modules over a six to 12 month period (half-day modules with 'homework' in between). Material = accessible and humorous. Topics: Ways to meet and greet customers; handling customer information enquiries; selling; handling complaints. We will create real case studies based on the customer research.*

Note: *We are not married to any particular methodology at this point. While this might seem somewhat 'loose', it represents customisation to Iarnród Éireann, not an 'off the shelf' design done for some other organisation.*

Outcome: *A real appetite to provide brilliant service.*

Phase 3 : Implement a 'Customer First' Culture: *"Execute relentlessly, learning from mistakes, knowing when to stick to the plan and when to modify"*

Key Questions/Steps

- *We need to find ways to embed customer service into the culture. Example: Have this as part of the Performance Management System.*

- *Action Learning Teams: Provide huge energy to tackle 'complex challenges'.*

- *Bottom-up Engagement: Identify 'local' solution that will really work. We will use the initial training programmes to gather ideas and suggestions from the staff and push them to resolve issues that lie within their own 'sphere of influence'.*

This is not simply a 'training' intervention but a way to really engage and energise staff at all organisational levels.

- *External Accreditation: It may be useful to look for some form of external accreditation for the work completed. This would provide a 'stamp of approval' and further underpin the direction. There are various training/change awards that we could tap into.*

- *Communications Mechanisms: To demonstrate real progress and to highlight 'heroes and customer service champions'.*

- *Training Workshops: A shared, positive experience for everyone in the company (senior executives, middle managers, all staff). Accessible, humorous and <u>real.</u>*

- *Measurement is a critical determinant of success. We need to establish a 'tracking system' that gives us feedback on 'how we are doing'. Exact criteria to be established.*

- *Address the 'rewards/recognition' lever — to give visibility to this programme. Lots of possibilities here for various forms of 'Oscars'.*

Outcome: *A dramatic change in the culture with a real focus on customer service.*

You are here! You now understand the underlying principles of organisation change. You have completed the planning phase and lined up your 'ducks in a row'. Using the Transformation Roadmap as a guide, you have selected key change targets. That is all the hard work completed, right? The implementation stage is going to be easy now that all the preparation is done? If only it were so …

CHANGE
IMPLEMENTATION:
HOW?

8

HUMAN RESPONSES TO CHANGE

Even if you have systematically worked through the earlier sections, the implementation phase has the potential to become the Achilles' heel of an organisation change programme. As one executive expressed it: "Implementation is where the rubber meets the sky".[40] Why is this the case? Up to this point, a lot of the planning has been completed 'behind closed doors', typically with senior people who are likely to benefit from the proposed changes. Now, they have to take this *car (which has been secretly designed in a locked garage)*, and see whether it will drive on the road. The logic of what you have worked on to date will now be tested.

Magnificent Five: Under the implementation heading, it is worthwhile to consider five implementation hurdles that need to be overcome in almost all change projects. While the specifics of each change project will determine their potency, these issues are always in play.

- **Understanding:** The psychology of change.
- **Building:** Senior team change capability.
- **Engaging:** Powerful individual and group connection strategies.
- **Convincing:** Getting some early wins on the board.
- **Reinforcing:** Copperfasten the new culture to ensure sustainability.

---

[40] Senior executive, insurance industry, speaking with the author, October 2011.

UNDERSTANDING: THE PSYCHOLOGY OF CHANGE

Reactions to Change: People's *reactions* to change normally can be grouped into one of three categories:

- The *method* of deciding/introducing change.
- The *content* of the specific change programme.
- The *psychological reaction* to change itself.

The *method* of deciding/introducing change

Where changes are imposed 'top down' with little consultation, staff typically feel they have no *control* over what is happening. In this scenario, they may react negatively, regardless of whether the change actually 'benefits' them. Several times, I have seen examples where companies introduced changes that resulted in improved job security or working conditions for staff. Yet, there is almost always pushback against the *imposition* of change. There is a strong cultural dimension to this – with particular change methods being more/less acceptable in different countries. The 'extreme' countries that I personally have worked in are Holland (where the need to involve staff is highest) and China (where the need to involve staff is lowest). Ireland ranks closer to the Dutch end of the spectrum, given our national 'anti-establishment' leaning. An old joke captures this. Following a shipwreck in the Pacific, an Irish guy manages to swim to the nearest island. When he meets a native, he says: "What's the government here? I'm against it!"

In my experience, people do not resist change — they resist *being changed*. It is as if someone in your family said: "Great news. I've typed up your New Year resolutions. You are going to lose weight, get fit and save money. It will be a really productive year for you". Not kosher. All other things being equal, taking a more participative path works best – a point covered in some depth earlier. However, the *caveat* remains that leaders sometimes need to impose change when the level of 'external threat' faced by the organisation is critical or where participative methods have been tried and failed. But, even in cases where change is forced, a later 're-build' phase normally follows.

One way to think about involvement is for the senior team to focus on *ends* rather than *means*. What is required is top management clarity around the end point — rather than a micro-managed exact sequence of steps to get there. Allowing groups to re-invent *their own wheel* may seem outwardly wasteful in terms of productivity. But this can make perfect organisation sense. Even prisons cannot be run without the co-operation of the inmates! Before and *during* change programmes, executives need to carefully listen to the workforce, to what is openly said and to what remains unspoken. Where the implementation phase is badly handled, all of the preparation work done in the preceding phases can simply unravel.

New CEOs: The most common trigger of a negative reaction is when a new CEO takes over an existing operation and decides to 'push through' a change programme. Philosophically, there is nothing wrong with a new leader deciding to launch a change initiative. However, 'how' this is achieved needs careful planning and execution:[41] 100% 'market share' simply is not available under this heading. Even the best planned and communicated change programmes will be resisted by *some* members of staff. The leadership role is to reduce, rather than to eliminate, the size of the opposition. Even where the method has been cleverly thought-through, the senior team need to steel themselves for a wave of unpopularity during the announcement of a change programme. As one CEO described it: "If you want to be liked, move out of management and get a job as an ice-cream salesman".[42]

The *content* of specific change programmes

People react to change in relation to how they believe it will impact them. They consider, consciously or subconsciously, the following:

---

[41] For an expanded discussion on 'successful entry strategies' for new CEOs, see Mooney, P. (2009). *Accidental Leadership*, Dublin: The Liffey Press.

[42] In conversation with the author, August 2011. This manager actually became very popular in the organisation – as he was seen to lead a major and necessary turnaround programme. The central point of course is that this popularity came as a 'by-product' of doing the right thing for the organisation. When popularity is sought for its own sake, it often proves ephemeral. Like a shadow, the more managers chase after it, the more it moves away.

- Does this change make sense? Is it a good idea?
- What are the benefits/disadvantages to me personally?
- Does this fit with my image/expectations of the organisation?
- Will I be able to do what is asked of me?
- Is this consistent with my values? (Am I being asked to do anything which I cannot support/believe in?)

CHALLENGING LITERACY IN A FOOD COMPANY

When we became involved in a major change programme in a food sector company (a supplier of ready-made meals), the barriers to change seemed particularly high. Under the proposed organisation structure, a layer of middle managers was being removed. Shop-floor workers would be empowered to make a range of decisions, provided that they followed Standard Operating Procedures, a normal control mechanism in the heavily-regulated food industry. After a lot of pushback, it emerged that low levels of literacy were at the root of a major fear – shop-floor staff would be exposed and labelled as stupid. The executive team were not aware of the literacy problem prior to the suggested changes and initially could not understand the vehement reaction, which included a three-day work stoppage.

Once the problem was understood (a union official uncovered the real issue), it was possible to put a proactive literacy-training programme in place and overcome this fear. Not everyone made it through the programme. Some staff moved into other roles in the organisation and some decided to leave. Interestingly, several of the shop-floor staff had not told their own children that they struggled with literacy and had been able to 'mask' this problem successfully over many years. They did not want to be outed by the suggested changes – either to the senior team or their own families.[43]

The *psychological* reaction to change itself

For most of us, *change* brings an element of discomfort. If you go on holidays to a new location, it often takes time to 'get your bearings' – to find good local restaurants, a safe beach for swimming, etc. Even a family holiday, where people have *chosen* to go to a new location, introduces changes that can be experienced as disruption. *Familiarity* is hardwired into most of us and acts like a comfort blanket. We see this in all spheres of life. "This is my local pub" (unspoken: *they know me; I am safe and comfortable here).* At a deeper level *resistance* to change can be understood as an *evaluation* stage – rather than simply *blind rejection.* Sigmund Freud argued that healthy individuals resist change *in order to protect themselves from an environment that they cannot easily handle or control.*[44] Viewed in this way, resistance is not an aberration, but a normal human reaction to change, to *newness.* Resistance actually has a functional value to prevent much that is valuable being swept away. The ultimate measure of the strength of resistance is time – with people becoming more accustomed to the suggested changes once they have had time to 'mentally work through this phase'.

Provided that a senior team follows the planning steps outlined earlier, the level of ambiguity associated with change programmes will be minimised. Being able to answer the question: "What exactly is going to happen next?" with a concrete response is a good starting point. But, regardless of the level of planning or communications expertise, it is impossible to completely eliminate the trauma of change. All change programmes are disruptive. Like travelling on the car ferry to

---

43   I have an interesting personal take on this. My own father was illiterate – having left school really early. I did not find out that he could not read or write until several years after he died.

44   Freud, S. (1962). *Three Essays on the Theory of Sexuality*, New York: Basic Books.

Liverpool, some crossings are smoother than others, but there is no way to completely eliminate rough water.

Change Responses: While the psychological reaction to change differs between individuals/groups, the most common reactions are these:[45]

- **Fear of the Unknown:** A feature of all organisational transitions is high uncertainty. Change arouses a fear of the *unknown*. People typically avoid situations that lack clarity or have an unknown probability of success. People need to know the future before *stepping forward* and often require a degree of stability and security. **Executive Role:** In earlier chapters, we touched on this point. All successful change management programmes need to ensure that 'tomorrow' is made as graphic and as emotionally appealing as possible. Critical executive role during this phase = *fog clearance.*

- **Need for Order:** Some people have an excessive need for order and symmetry. They are unable to tolerate disorder or confusion. The ambiguity surrounding change programmes leads to anxiety, which in turn lowers performance. **The Risk:** At a time of change, *more* work is required as the organisation continues with the 'today job' and battles to move towards its new *modus operandi*. The contradiction is that staff can get completely distracted by internal politics and endless scenario discussions. At a time when more outputs are required, staff can actually be producing less. **Executive Role:** In reality, change = disorder. Despite the 'best laid plans', it is not always possible to anticipate what lies ahead. The way to overcome this is to continually create 'short-term certainty': "I don't know the answer to your question about the developing situation in Indonesia, but this is what I need you to focus on in the next month. As soon as I know more about our major raw materials supplier in Indonesia, I will let you know. Either way, we will meet again to look at this four weeks from now. But, let me re-

---

[45] Of course, some individuals and groups relish change and none of these responses will be evident. But these are the most common reactions we have encountered in working through change programmes.

stress. This is what I want you to focus on over the next couple of weeks ...".

- **Fear of Failure:** Some people avoid taking risks, even settle for less in order to avoid the pain of failing. In the early phases of transition, some people resist change because they have developed patterns for coping with the present situation and are reluctant to develop new patterns that may not be successful. Resistance to change, which can outwardly seem like an effort to avoid the pain or discomfort often associated with change, sometimes masks a fear of failure. Like a teenager refusing to sit the Leaving Certificate exams ("I just can't be bothered"), staff feel that if they do not 'commit' then they cannot fail. **Executive Role:** Executive teams need to *demonstrate* confidence – be crystal clear on what exactly is going to happen and the support that staff will receive to help them cope in the new environment. The key here is *doing*, not *talking*. Providing training in *bite-sized chunks* delivered in a 'fun way' can be hugely helpful. Assisting staff when they are faced with obstacles (and acknowledging the progress they are actually making) also is interpreted as being supportive. People tend to overly focus on the climb ahead. The executive task is to show them the amount of the mountain that has already been conquered!

- **Sense of Loss:** Part of the discomfort of moving through a change programme can stem from a sense of 'loss' for what used to be. For some people, *yesterday* is a more comfortable place mentally than *tomorrow*. We tend to stereotype older people as always looking backwards (Dublin in the rare oul' times) – but the same rearview-mirror psychology can apply to people of all ages. There can be significant romantic nostalgia for the 'old company' and how good it was to work there, a false memory much like we remember all the great summer weather when we were growing up. In some ways, staff are saying: "Can we turn the world back to the way it used to be? I liked *that* world more that I like *this* new world you are describing." **Executive Role:** It is worth considering a 'ritual' that allows people to let go of the past in a respectful way.

Executives can draw inspiration from anthropology here. This is the equivalent of having an 'official funeral' (burial ceremony) for the old organisation to help staff to move forward. In one US example, staff from two 'merging companies' were asked to bring along a memento of the old organisation (a pen, paperweight, letterhead, etc.). These items were placed in a coffin and buried in the grounds of the new HQ – with a headstone to denote the 'passing' of the old organisation. Not 100% sure that this particular technique would be a big hit in Termonfeckin – but you get the overall point. All too often, new CEOs want to dismiss past achievements and concentrate on 'what's broken'. It is usually an 'entry error' – highlighting the new executive's own anxiety as much as the past sins of the organisation.

Allow Time: These psychological reactions occur because an individual is passing through a personal transition. In this context, most change is stressful. A promotion can be as stressful, albeit perhaps not in such a traumatic way, as being made redundant. People move through a transition phase with different degrees of difficulty, but most will pass through it in some way. I always caution executive teams to 'slow down their expectations' at the front-end of a change programme. Provided that the changes make sense, the majority of staff will come round to supporting the logic. There is almost always a small group of staff who will be pulled 'dragging and screaming' through the process and who may never acknowledge the necessity for change. Some people 'couldn't be happy in heaven' and senior teams will never convince all of the people, all of the time. But, over time, most people will work through a change process successfully. The executive team often forget their own initial reaction to proposed changes – sometimes a similar degree of scepticism – but they have had time to work through this before the changes are announced to the staff. Employees need time to undertake a similar journey, a journey towards acceptance. Do not panic. Batten down the hatches. This too will pass!

Speeding Up: The psychology of managing change does not have any 'tricks' to speed up acceptance. While it may be somewhat boring, you simply need to cover off on the *basics*. Allow staff to *understand* the current situation in terms of having access to the facts and appropriate information. Communicate the core *rationale* – the need to change (because the *status quo* is not sustainable, because the organisation is moving to a better place or both). Support the development of *skills*, which allows staff to perform in the new environment. Put rocket fuel onto staff *motivation* where you can demonstrate that there is a personal upside in the change programme (higher skills levels, job security, etc).

9

BUILDING SENIOR TEAM CHANGE CAPABILITY

Ensuring that the management team has the motivation and skills to lead a change programme is the second 'big issue' in the implementation phase of a change programme. To bring this to life, we will review two very different case studies. In the first case (Bord Na Móna), the 'what needs to be done' question was crystal clear. The executive team had already devised a new strategy and our role as consultants was simply to help implement this. In the second case ('PaperCo'), the presenting issues were much less certain. The case describes our approach to 'fog clearance', helping to find the best route forward. Before we consider these cases in detail, it is worthwhile to make a couple of general points under the heading of building senior team capability.

Change Skills: Change initiatives often fail because managers are not equipped with the skills required to manage in the new environment. Yet, amazingly, ensuring that the management team has the necessary skills to manage the 'new' operation is often completely overlooked. While the senior team may be able to run the existing business well, it does not automatically follow that they have the skills to manage a large-scale change process. The unspoken assumption is often: the management team is smart, let them go figure. This is a high-risk option underpinned by a flawed logic. Managing change is not 'business-as-usual'. By implication, it is 'business-as-unusual' and several new skills may be required that are not normally in play. You would not ask a GP to perform open-heart surgery – not because he or she is not smart – but because they are not trained in that particular specialism. Similarly, managers need to be trained in the skills required to manage change. What is the downside if you don't do this?

Sometimes the result of throwing people in at the deep end is a condition called 'drowning'.

Competency *precedes* **Commitment:** Much of the published material on organisational change holds that, in order to introduce change, you need to first win 'the hearts and minds' of the workforce.[46] Our experience is the exact opposite. Behaviours are a much more potent target than attitudes. Change programmes should concentrate on roles, responsibilities and relationships rather than on attitudes. If these can be changed, the attitudes will follow.

Competency leads to commitment – not the other way around. A significant sub-benefit of this approach is that it maintains a concrete link with reality. When you talk to a supervisory or middle management group about 'changing the organisation culture', you can see them almost visibly switch-off. It is much better to be *concrete* – for example, focus on reducing throughput time by 50% and teach them process mapping and diagnostic skills to achieve this. **Central Idea:** You can change the culture of an organisation without ever using the term.

Top Down: Change starts at the top; a management team that is lukewarm about change will not convince the staff to make the 'great leap forward'. And *convincing* staff typically does not happen at the 'big staged events' – the Town Hall meetings (sometimes labelled 'Come to Jesus' sessions) with the CEO. It happens on the night-shift, in sidebar conversations in the canteen or the locker room. The big events are useful to help communicate what is happening and why. But, it is the local managers in small pockets of the organisation that get the ball over the line. That is why you need the middle management team on your side in this debate, acting as hidden persuaders in the change process.

---

[46] An 'engagement strategy' does not apply in every sphere. The exact author of the quote: "When you've got them by the balls, their hearts and minds will soon follow" is uncertain, although it is reputed to have been on the wall in the office of Charles Colson during his service in the Nixon Administration (*circa* 1972). However, it is likely to have predated Colson. Given the general belief that the saying related to the Vietnam War, it seems likely that it originated during the President Johnson era, possibly a quote from Henry Kissinger.

Tough Calls: In any 'new game', some managers will find it difficult to play at a higher standard and not everyone will make it. The organisation has to walk an ultra-thin line here. While the usual message to staff (including managers) is one of support, helping them to adjust to the new scenario, recalcitrant individuals cannot stall momentum. One author described these managers as: 'The type of person who quit your company two years ago, but just hasn't left yet'.[47] Where a manager is blocking progress, the initial focus is to understand why the individual is not performing at the expected level or seems reluctant to embrace the 'new way'. You cannot fix a problem that you do not understand and sometimes resistance is based on a legitimate counterview that is *always* worth listening to (it may be a philosophical objection, the manager could be struggling to perform at the new level, etc.). Underperformance can occur for a variety of reasons – and you need to drill into the details to fully understand this before making the call.

Within General Electric, a decision-matrix is used to help pinpoint the reasons for managerial underperformance. The matrix (see **Figure 12**) categorises managers into performing and underperforming groups – and also differentiates between those who *share* and those who *do not share* the organisation values. This provides a relatively simple method to categorise the current group of managers and offers a fine-grained response to underperformance, a more sophisticated response than *dragging someone around the back of the factory and having them shot*. A similar analysis of the overall management team can be a useful starting point to change management programmes. Like Alex Ferguson contemplating the coming season, you need to be sure that all of the key positions have been correctly filled.

---

[47]   Claybaugh, W. (2009). *The Be Nice Revolution*, North Mankato, MN: Capstone Publishing.

Figure 12: The General Electric Management Team Assessment Model

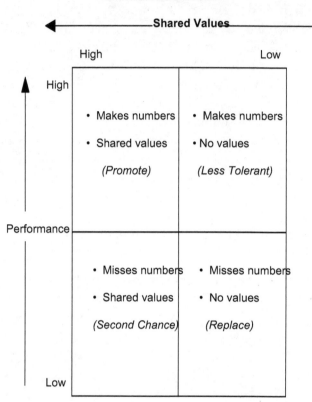

Changing Horses: At some point in the process, organisations need to give up on the 'change journey' with individuals and ask them to leave the organisation. The message to your management team should be simple. 'If you find it difficult to lead this initiative, then at least you need to support it. If you cannot either lead or support the change initiative, you need to get out of the way'. The rule is simple: "If you can't change the people, change the people". Once the initial debates have been worked through, there is zero room for second-guessing or 'nay-saying'. The role for the CEO typically is to tell the team: "Get on board for this because there will be no spectators on the pitch".

SKILLING UP: BORD NA MÓNA

Bord Na Móna is an intriguing organisation. Closely associated in the public mind with the production of peat briquettes (using compressed peat as fuel for domestic heating), in practice the business spans a number of areas including fuels, horticulture, energy and the environment.

Historically Innovative: *Bord Na Móna holds a special place in the history of Organisation Development in Ireland. The company had successfully experimented with autonomous work teams in the 1960s and 1970s – using a socio-technical work systems approach pioneered by the Tavistock Institute in the UK. But, this early experimentation eventually fizzled out. In common with many of the semi-State organisations in Ireland, slowness to change became a defining part of the culture. Underpinning this was a strong sense of job security. The company had 'been around forever' (in fact, for 75 years); in the minds of staff, this would continue into the future. There were few sanctions or rewards available to the senior team to help them drive performance.*

Enter the Dragon: *When a new CEO, Gabriel Darcy, was appointed in February 2008, he began a major change programme. A strategic vision for the organisation (New Contract with Nature) was developed based on a radically different organisation strategy. He wanted to diversify the organisation, on the basis that the traditional business markets were declining. He was looking for opportunities to move into areas where the core strengths of the company could be used. Darcy had 'served his time' in the army and later worked for Kerry Foods. His enthusiastic, hard charging style was new to Bord Na Móna and not universally liked. He was well aware of the concept that 'you have to break eggs to make omelettes' and was not unduly concerned about personal popularity. He was much more exercised about the length of time it was taking to* 'turn the tanker' of a diverse organisation that employed thousands of people across a huge number of locations.

New Blood: *A key initial step was the external hiring of a couple of senior players. A mixture of home-grown and external talent was formed into a tightly-knit 'kitchen cabinet'. It was this group who subsequently developed the change agenda – a bold and exciting future vision for the organisation based on the central theme of environmental sustainability. In the semi-State sector, this was heady stuff, certainly well beyond 'yesterday +10%'. Inevitably, some of the wider management team were sceptical that this new vision actually could be realised.*

Executive Development: *A key part of the 'moving forward' strategy was to ensure that the extended management team (about 80 people) would be fully skilled to make the change journey. Tandem Consulting won the contract to design and deliver a comprehensive Executive Development Programme to underpin the overall change efforts. While a detailed discussion is outside the scope of this book, a summary version of the programme is detailed below. A key design element was applied-learning 'work projects' – making sure that the new skills would be brought to bear on resolving real-life work issues faced by the participants. Adults learn by doing, not by hearing about how things are done. Systematic executive development was a cornerstone in the overall change efforts. At the time of writing, this initiative is still underway – so it is too soon to crow about success. But the early indicators (based on a range on internal metrics) are certainly positive.*

Structured Inquiry: *As part of the programme design, we[48] asked the extended management team what we needed to focus on. We used this questionnaire:*

---

[48]   Dermot Rush, Cathy Buffini and Paul Dooley led this particular initiative. My own involvement in the design of this instrument was peripheral. But I am happy to hog some of the credit for their talent!

Name:

Division:

Position:

Introduction: Thank you for your time. Your input and suggestions will be invaluable in helping us to design the programme. This brief survey should take approx 30 minutes to complete. Before Bord Na Móna runs the 2012 Leadership Development Programme, we need to understand the specific needs of the business, the work environment and the culture around managing people. The questions start at the broad business level and work down into a more specific exploration of critical skills and competencies. Please add anything else you feel would help us design and deliver a high-impact development programme.

Part 1: Strategic & Business Level

What are the Critical Success Factors [CSFs] needed to deliver the Bord Na Móna strategy?

What skills do managers need to demonstrate to deliver the strategy?

What are the current strengths of this business?

What are the most challenging weaknesses or 'gaps' within the business?

What, if anything, is inhibiting change? What needs to change in order to achieve the strategy?

What key challenges are facing your **individual** business?

Of the challenges listed (across the total organisation and within your own business), what is the single most important issue to address?

Part 2: Operational & Work Environment

What brings the best out in people in the current Bord Na Móna work environment?

What, if anything, inhibits this?

How would you describe the current management style and organisation culture?

Is this working? How could it be improved?

Part 3: People & Competencies

What behaviours for success/competencies will be key to Bord Na Móna's future success?

Are there unrealised capabilities and potential? In what areas?

Do you feel middle managers are currently operating to their full potential?

Where do you feel managers (and teams) need most support to achieve their objectives?

Part 4: The Development Programme

Bord Na Móna is about to embark on a significant investment in developing managers. The aim is to equip managers with the critical capabilities for running the business. We want learning to 'stick' and to have a significant positive impact on the business. Getting the design right is critical.

What do you see as the main areas to address in how your people currently perform?

> *Knowledge?*

> *Skills?*

> *Attitudes?*

> *Behaviours?*

Can you prioritise the following areas in terms of importance to Bord Na Móna from a programme content perspective: (rank from 1 to 8)

> *Managing and facilitating change*

> *Negotiation and influencing people*

> *Operational excellence & process improvement*

> *Business scorecards and other measurement metrics*

> *Coaching for performance*

> *Team development and facilitation*

> *Dealing with underperformance*

> *Personal authenticity in leadership*

> *Something else?*

Can you think of any specific areas where business improvement initiatives (micro-projects) would be helpful within your area?

Would you be willing to sponsor a micro-project? Yes? __No? __

What indicators will show this programme has had the desired effect? What will improve? What will change? Be as specific as possible.

Overall, on a scale of 1 to 10 (1 being extremely poor and 10 being exemplary leadership), how would you rate the current level of leadership and managerial competence within the target participants of the programme in your business unit?

Is there anything else you would like to add here to ensure this development programme has the most positive and sustainable impact possible?

Thank you very much. The Tandem Team

The Core Curriculum: Once we had processed the data from the questionnaires, the curriculum for the *Leadership for Results* programme in Bord Na Móna was constructed as follows:

Figure 13: Leadership for Results Programme, Bord na Móna

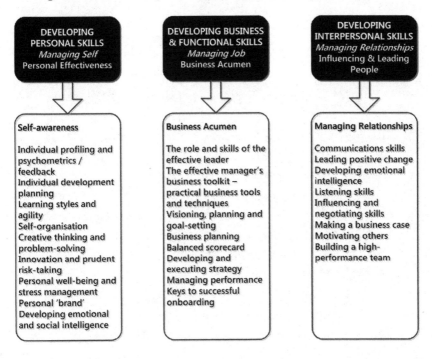

Centrality of Managers: Peter Drucker, arguably the world's foremost thinker on executive processes, said: "Managers are the engine of a business".[49] Declan Ryan, CEO of Irlandia and the patron of the One Foundation, expressed this slightly more colourfully: "Bad management gives me cancer".[50] Both recognised the central role that executives play in high performance organisations. In relation to managing change programmes, it is critically important to get the senior team 'on board' to drive it forward. We really see the potency of this in the negative. Where the senior team is 'not sold' on the benefits of a change programme, the likelihood of forward movement is on par with making ice cream in a furnace. The good news for chief executives is that the methods used to engage the senior team are exactly the same as getting the general workforce on board. Managers are not some 'sub-species' of the human race to which a different set of psychological rules apply. However, sometimes figuring out *why* the senior team is less than fully engaged can be difficult and needs to be carefully 'unpacked'. To illustrate this point, let us look at an actual example in a company that we will call PaperCo.

RELUCTANT EXECUTIVES: PAPERCO

> **Background:** *When a new CEO was appointed to this manufacturing company, I was asked to get involved to help enhance the performance of the plant. The starting point was to take a 'Polaroid snapshot' of what currently existed. There was lots of 'good news' to report. The management team seemed to have good potential for the future (average age was 36). Two of the direct reports were women and all were graduates. So far, so good; it looked like we had good raw material to work with. The new CEO also believed that there was a big prize available, in*

49   Drucker, P. (1993). *The Effective Executive*, New York: Harper Business Essentials.
50   In conversation with the author, June 2011.

terms of dramatic market share growth and new product potential in Ireland. There was a definite 'upside' in getting the senior team turbo-charged, assuming we could find the extra gear in the car. The senior team got on pretty well – so there were no chemistry issues that limited potential performance. Yet, the strong view of the CEO was that this group was "punching below their weight". The case started out as a mystery that needed to be resolved.

Geography Focus: *Historically, this group was managed from the UK. For some time, there had been no Managing Director at the Irish site and each of the functions reported directly into the UK as a cost-saving measure. For a variety of reasons, this structure had not worked well and led to declining performance levels until the decision was eventually made to appoint a CEO for the Irish operation. During the period when the group was directly managed from the UK, the senior team's appetite to take a more proactive role in the organisation dampened.* *Example:* *The site in Dublin was landlocked and blocking future growth potential. The management team should have considered moving to a greenfield site. But this, and many similar decisions, was in limbo awaiting the new CEO's arrival. The group effectively had become disempowered.*

How did this group 'see' their role? The CEO felt strongly that the senior team was not performing at the appropriate level. They essentially saw themselves as a 'middle management' team and did not envision their roles being performed at a higher level. For example, the Manufacturing Director (technically, an extremely capable guy), was responsible for all production activity on site. There were a number of technology and product enhancement opportunities, but he seemed happy to 'sail along' under the existing system. The HR Director was in the same mode (described by the CEO as "chug along"), failing to tackle inefficient workforce practices. The appetite to move the organisation up a gear to the next level of performance was a missing ingredient. Overall, there was a sense of complacency, based on the unspoken belief: "We are doing well". At the time, the company was making circa €1.3m per month in operating profits. Within the wider group (the parent company had a presence in 30+ countries), the Irish operations were seen as both profitable and efficient, which explained some of the complacency. However, the internal standards were poor and the company were underperforming vis-á-vis external competitors. I was able to source this external benchmark information and this became part of our 'armoury' to tackle complacency at the Irish site.

Questions Business: *Sometimes, consultants are in the 'questions' rather than the 'answers' business. After an initial trawl through the operation, the following questions were tabled for discussion with the new CEO:*

Question # 1: Understand 'what's happening here?'

The first step in effective problem solving is diagnosis – we need to fully understand what is happening. Even if we accept the basic premise that the group is underperforming, we need to ask: "Why is this the case?". In general terms, people do not perform because of one (or some combination) of three underlying issues

1. People do not perform because they do not know what is expected (lack of clarity around expectations or sometimes an educational issue).

Example: *Look at the history of this group. If a group of managers have become used to operating in a particular 'mode', this becomes the norm for them. If they have spent a lot of their working life in organisations where they were disempowered (in authoritarian organisations), they may not have been expected to take the lead or may even have been punished for doing this. Some managerial groups exhibit behaviour that can be labelled 'learned helplessness'. They do not really believe that they are empowered and organisations send mixed signals on this ("I want you to show initiative. Just be sure to clear any stuff with* me in advance"). How has the period of time when this group reported directly into the UK impacted them?

2. People do not perform because they do not know how (lack of skills or particular competencies).

Example: A group of managers may never have been involved in a strategic change project. If you then ask this group to be more 'strategic', they may not even know where to start (it is not a question of intelligence, just a lack of prior exposure and confidence). On an individual level, some managers are simply not proactive (they may be good managers but have little leadership ability – they may not seek to change the status quo).

3. People do not perform because they do not want to (lack of motivation).

Example: Lack of motivation comes in many guises. Stunted career ambition, laziness, sometimes a perception of not being in the 'inner circle'. In the new CEO's view, the 'remuneration packages' are not an issue. Would the senior managers agree with this? It is often useful to consider this issue in relation to the individual managers in the group. What are they individually looking for? What would represent a win for each of them out of this project?

Question # 2: Entire group or individuals within the group?

Is it your belief that the group 'as a whole' needs to step up a gear or would it be better to work with specific individuals? For example, using the performance management system, it might be possible to put specific 'growth/development' targets in place for individual managers.

Question # 3: Planning change with the total group or a smaller team?

Would you work with some of this group as an 'inner circle' to develop a change plan? One of the arguments for doing this is *the fact that currently there is a lot of other stuff underway. This option would 'cut down' on the level of involvement across the entire group (but has the obvious downside of the creation of an 'inner' and an 'outer' circle). It is quite a small team, so it would be difficult to do this without some members of the team feeling like they were being relegated to 'second cousin' status.*

Question # 4: Work to an agreed organisation change format?

*There are a number of potential 'models' of organisation change that organisations can use. A model I have developed (Managing Large Scale Organisational Change) is detailed below (**Figure 14**).[51]*

Question # 5: You provide the leadership and delegate the 'making it happen'.

Some CEOs see the crafting of strategy as essentially their role; the 'operationalisation' of this then is completed by the function managers. In essence, they believe that strategy development should be divorced from strategy execution. Sometimes this is 'personality-driven' (CEOs who are more comfortable with the big picture and less interested in detail); sometimes, it is tactical (they want to keep the management team's nose to the grindstone or may not have the managerial talent available, people who can be effective at the strategy level). Divorcing strategy from execution is not a view I share, but it is worth exploring.

---

[51]   This is an example of an approach to change that I had been using. This, and a variety of other models, eventually morphed into the Transformation Roadmap that forms the cornerstone of this book.

Figure 14: Managing Large Scale Organisational Change Model

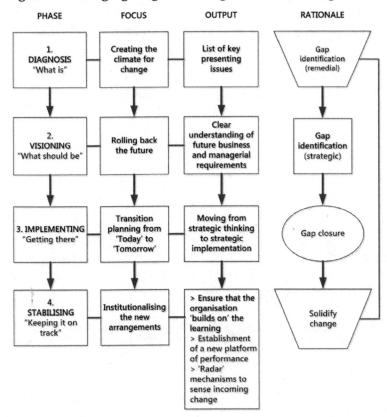

What Actually Happened? *The new CEO (a very competent player) worked through each of these questions until we had a solid understanding of the current situation. He then introduced the topic of organisation change to the entire management team. Over the next 18 months, the CEO led a very significant change programme at the plant that had an enormous impact on performance.* **The Lesson:** *'Being slow at the front-end' really worked. He did not race down the hill to announce: "Look at me. I've arrived. Everything is going to change here".*[52] *He took the time to get the senior team on board and they subsequently led*

---

52   For a more robust discussion on new CEO 'entry strategies', see Mooney, P. (1999). *Accidental Leadership*, Dublin: The Liffey Press.

the change programme from the front. If ever there was a case that demonstrated that managing change is 'more art than science', this was it. Having the managerial nous to know when to run fast and when to slow down is central to the successful planning and execution of change programmes. It is brilliant to see it done well and this was a perfect example of 'making haste slowly'.

❖ ❖ ❖ ❖ ❖

Nailing their Colours: I have seen a couple of methods that attempt to force the management team to 'sign up' for change programmes. One such checklist is detailed below.[53] The idea here is that individual managers *self-rate* on how they feel about a forthcoming change programme.

-5	-4	-3	-2	-1	+1	+2	+3	+4	+5
Antagonistic	Really Don't Believe in it	Mildly Negative	Uninterested: No Change	Probably Won't Resist	Will Go Along	Interested	Supportive	Strongly Supportive	Enthusiastic Advocate

Does it work? As a stand-alone idea, this type of checklist has very little merit. Very few managers who rate themselves at the lower end of the scale would openly admit this. But as a 'sensing mechanism', helping to *tease out* the general mood of a management team or their level of comfort with a suggested change programme, it could play a minor role. **Example:** If a senior team has just announced a major change programme to the extended management team, this type of

---

53 This checklist was in a pack of materials received on an Organisational Development training programme in the USA. The original source was not listed in the materials.

checklist can be used to gauge their initial reaction. The key to making this work is to have the session carefully facilitated. In many organisations, there is a deference to hierarchy. Picture the boardroom scene: A new CEO arrives and says: "This is what I am planning to do. It makes perfect sense. Now what do you think about my plan?". It requires a brave soldier to point out flaws in the General's plan. My overall sense is always to try to uncover the points of opposition to a change plan and the reasons underpinning this. Knowledge is power. When you understand these, you have some chance of addressing the viewpoints, even where these are counter to the proposed trajectory. Checklists, or some other method of facilitated session, legitimise counter viewpoints and allow these to be heard rather than being driven underground.

Critique, Do Not Criticise: Skilled consultants help the extended management team to understand the difference between 'critiquing' and 'criticising' a change programme – by openly listening to alternative viewpoints and creating forums for real discussion. All dissention is legitimate 'within the room'. But once the team make a decision and move outside this forum, they must show a united front. It is the equivalent of 'Cabinet responsibility' in politics. While individual ministers may disagree with a particular policy initiative, they must show a solid front to the electorate. And the message to all managers around this principle must be stark: managers who want to 'run with the hare and chase with the hounds' eventually will find themselves out of a job and telling all of the people on the dole queue how they could have saved the world and other interesting stories! Harsh? Perhaps, but this is *realpolitik* in organisation life. As a manager, you cannot accept the role, the salary and the perks without the requisite responsibilities. And those leading change programmes need to emphasise this – to ensure that there is no doubt as to what is expected from the senior and extended management team.

In terms of managing change programmes, you cannot be 'a little bit pregnant'. This is a tough, all-or-nothing climb, in which the management team plays a centrally important role. Ultimately, organisations are not run on a democratic basis. Managers cannot decide to 'opt out' on leading change programmes from the front.

Ensuring that they have the competence and the commitment *to* lead change programmes is an important success factor. Management is a key resource in leading change programmes and every effort needs to be made to build capability. **Figure 15** captures some of the strategies that organisations can use to strengthen this key group.

Figure 15: Strategies for Building Managerial Capability[54]

Strategy	Definition	Today's Score (1 low/10 high)	Actions to Improve
Buy	Acquire new talent by recruiting individuals from outside the organisation or from other departments.		
Build	Train or develop talent through education, formal job training, job rotation, job assignments and action learning.		
Benchmark	Visit organisations that excel in work processes that we have targeted for improvement. What can we learn?		
Borrow	Partner with consultants, vendors, customers, or suppliers outside the firm to garner new ideas or utilise short-term assignments.		
Bounce	Remove low-performing or underperforming individuals.		
Bind	Retain the most talented employees.		

ENGAGING: POWERFUL INDIVIDUAL AND GROUP CONNECTION STRATEGIES

Most change projects start with noble aspirations – delivering *sustainable* change and a legacy of high performance. In the preceding section, we have demonstrated the importance of 'getting managers involved in the mix'. How this is achieved is critically important. Like

---

[54] I came across an earlier version of this model about 20 years ago. It has been modified over time. The original source of the model has been 'lost in space'.

the old Kodak advertisement said: "The genius is in the details". While there is never an explicit goal to disempower the line management team, this is sometimes an unintended consequence of involving external consultants in scoping change programmes. So the first hurdle to be overcome is not 'how to motivate' the management team but 'how to avoid de-motivating them'.

Unintended Consequence: An unexpected outcome of using consultants is that the line management team can feel ignored and pushed out of the centre of activity. Consultants (especially if they are working on a fixed price contract) typically want to get *in-and-out*. They complete the diagnosis, highlighting the critical issues and what needs to be done. They then either hand over the implementation to the local management team or stay *in situ* and direct operations. This doctor-patient approach has a number of potential flaws. At a surface level, managers often feel that "Consultants ask us what's wrong and how to fix it, package what we say and then leave with a shedload of money". It is hard to motivate a senior team who believe that their ideas have been stolen and they have not received the credit, financial or otherwise. But, the problem of bypassing the local management team is deeper than a *poor morale* issue.

Smart Clients: Using the inherent capabilities within the client organisation makes perfect sense. **Example**: Where an 'action learning' approach to managing change is used, the management team and the consulting group complete various tasks and subsequently reflect on the outcomes. This simple method of taking time out acts like a half-time dressing-room analysis in a football match. It can equip leadership teams with the necessary 'insights' to modify change initiatives.

A change management approach based on this philosophy *engages* leaders and teams throughout each step of the change process. Internal managers sit 'at the top table' during the early planning discussions (some consulting approaches exclude the line management team from this). And, as each critical phase unfolds, managers (sometimes more junior staff are present also) are engaged around overcoming obstacles. It provides the confidence to drive future changes internally – using the resources of the organisation rather than overly relying on consultants. This is engagement in practice; real work brings the concept of empowerment alive – and the management team are the first target audience for this. Let us be honest here. It is impossible for any consulting group to 'ride in on a white horse' and, after a couple of days, understand 100 years of organisation history, complex product lines, nuances of culture and key competitor moves. Such an approach, which is overly reliant on consulting inputs, puts a huge burden on the external team and ignores the experience that resides within the current organisation. It is smarter to 'marry' the expertise of the consulting group with the knowledge and ability that exists internally.

ENGAGEMENT PROCESSES: GETTING THE STAFF ON BOARD[55]

Large organisations normally have a number of different processes by which employees can become involved in issues affecting their work and the services provided. **Figure 16** summarises a range of employee engagement processes. Such processes are commonly categorised as 'direct' and 'representative'. Direct forms of engagement provide employees with opportunities to become involved as individuals – for example, *via* appraisal systems, climate surveys, project teams and so on. In representative forms of engagement, employees take part through the mediating role of their trade union representatives, information and consultation systems, collective bargaining, formal partnership committees, etc.

While some organisations may provide exclusively direct or indirect forms of employee engagement, many make both forms available to employees, sometimes by choice and sometimes to comply with legal obligations (often referred to as 'mixed forms' of engagement). But we need to insert a *caveat*. Having the 'structures in place' to engage with staff really tells very little about the effectiveness of the engagement

---

[55] Dr. John O'Dowd in Tandem Consulting developed the central model outlined in this section. John's view is that are many ways to collect data around engagement levels. Where the numbers are large, it often makes sense to use an online survey method, alongside one-on-one meetings with senior players and focus groups to help understand the emotions behind the numbers. Using a range of methods provides both qualitative and quantitative data.

efforts. The level of engagement is determined by the fundamental engagement *philosophy* in place.

Figure 16: Employee Engagement Processes

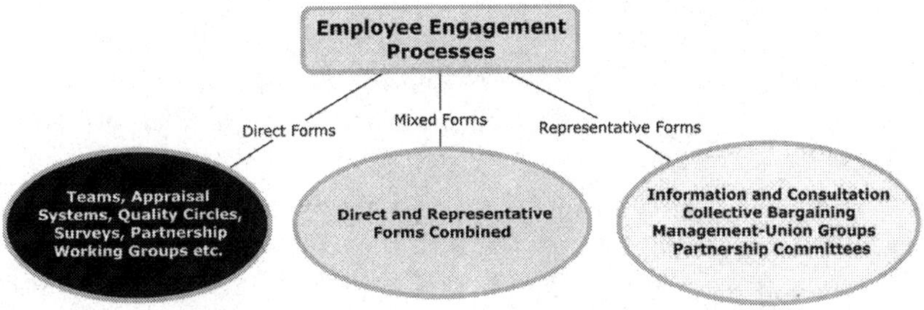

Engagement Philosophies: Organisations approach the engagement question from different philosophical starting points. Some use engagement simply as a mechanism to *lower resistance* to change. Consider the following example: Unless you work in a kibbutz, 'one person, one vote' is not the culture in most organisations. The management team is in control and expected to lead. But simply 'telling' people what to do only gets them into third gear – not turbo-charged. The leadership genius is to release the *discretionary* commitment of staff, essentially *winning without the war*. Depending on the complexity of the individual business, it can be difficult to communicate a boardroom concept to the shop-floor in a way that inspires positive action and it is all too easy for messages to get 'lost in translation'. However, when the future vision evolves from the members of the organisation themselves (through engagement), communications and implementation hurdles get swept aside. The underpinning goal in this scenario is to use engagement as a 'mechanism to lower resistance to change'.

Beyond Resistance: An alternative view is that engaging the workforce has benefits far and above simply 'lowering resistance'. Some organisations believe that employees should be involved in co-creating the future to release their creativity. I have seen this expressed as: "The senior team doesn't have a monopoly on good ideas" and as: "None of us is as smart as all of us". To be effective, this philosophy should be not simply be dusted off during times of change, but should be an ongoing feature within the organisation. For example, 3M, the company best-known for the creation of yellow Post-it notes, recognises staff potential in a host of ways, including encouraging staff to 'bootleg' up to 10% of their time to work on new products. The slogan: "Every employee comes to work equipped with a mind ... at absolutely no extra cost" – captures this idea of tapping into workforce creativity. While 3M is genuinely committed to this, in some organisations' slogans simply represent clever wordsmithing – a tribute to slick writing rather than a fundamental belief in staff engagement. Real engagement goes well beyond sloganising. It follows that engaging staff during change programmes is not equally open to all organisations. Organisations that have previously used this method (not just in times of crisis) have an obvious advantage in terms of being able to quickly tap into workforce commitment when 'all hands' are needed on the oars.

Engagement: What are You Trying to Achieve? Engagement is an emerging part of the modern manager's toolkit. Historically, most companies operated hierarchical organisations, fashioned after the 'military model', which focused on role clarity and demanded obedience. In a combat situation, there is no mileage in lack of clarity or insubordination. Under this model, a number of assumptions (often unconscious, mostly unspoken) were held including:

- Management's job is to *manage* (plan, organise, lead and control).[56] In contrast, a workers job was to *do* – sometimes referred to as the *inspired* and the *perspired*.

- Management education gave people the skills and tools needed to run a business. Workers' education gave people the skills to carry out specific tasks. When something went *wrong*, it was primarily the managerial role to fix this.

- Absenteeism, labour turnover, grievances, high overtime practices were all driven by the underlying fact that workers wanted to do *as little work as possible* for *as much reward as*

---

[56] Based on the often-quoted definition of management by Henri Fayol. This French mining engineer was one of the first people to put forward a general theory of management.

possible. It followed that the workforce needed to be closely supervised and controlled.

High-engagement Work Systems: Over the past number of years, a number of the assumptions in the above have been challenged and even 'turned on their heads'. Some of the emerging beliefs include:

- Most people want to contribute to the success of the organisation and, if given the opportunity, will do so.
- Managerial skills (for example, problem-solving) can be learned quite easily by most people.
- People now come to work with a different expectation around how they should be treated. Most new recruits grew up in 'democratic families' (their first experience of organisation). Younger employees (classified as either Generation X or Generation Y depending on their date of birth) bring an expectation of democracy to work and reject authoritarianism.
- The consumer focus on product and service quality (now seen as a *given)* means that everyone in the workforce needs to be engaged around service delivery (it is not solely the prerogative of a small group who are responsible for quality).
- People are 'oil gushers' of creativity and can come up with great solutions to internal problems if the organisation climate is conducive to this (have another look at the GE Workout model, detailed earlier, which underpins this).

Beyond the Traditional Model: Some companies have long since moved beyond the 'traditional model'. In such organisations (for example, Hewlett-Packard, Ulster Bank, Marks & Spencer,[57] Motorola, Royal Bank of Scotland), the link between employee satisfaction/engagement and productively is taken as an article of faith – and is measured annually. In more traditional organisations, the link between engaging employees and improved productivity is tenuous and needs to be *proven* to the management team. In these organisations, the *business case* for engaging employees needs to be

---

[57] In 2011, Marks & Spencer reported an engagement score of 75% with an employee survey response rate of 95%. *Source: People Management*, CIPD, 2011.

made by proponents of the view that this provides an 'extra gear of performance'. My strong belief is that engagement works best when employees are working on real-life challenges. Simplifying an existing process or responding to a price threat in the marketplace are examples of 'real work'. While summer picnics and Christmas parties are great, these should be additive – not a substitute for engaging staff on substantive organisational issues.

Engagement Model: Even if a company is sold on the idea that engaging staff provides a real organisational benefit, the 'how' of engagement can be confusing. To help make this concept clearer, I have developed a model that shows how the various ideas are linked. Using specific examples helps to 'bring the concept alive' – particularly to groups of line managers who can be sceptical about 'touchy feely' ideas (see **Figure 17**).

Don't Over-Eat: There is no suggestion that an organisation would attempt to do *everything* listed – that is, work on all '20' items. The individual ideas detailed in the model should be treated as a 'menu of options', from which the management team choose ideas that will work in their specific environment. It is usually a combination of *something old and something new*. Only *greenfield* organisations are starting from scratch and can decide their culture in advance. In *brownfield* organisations, the engagement model will help you to figure out which current systems need to be re-energised alongside some completely new concepts that can add additional value.

Key Question: "Do I *belong* to a *noble* organisation and *share* in its success?". **Central Point:** Unless the answer to the basic question posed above is "Yes", the more advanced engagement methods will not have full impact. In essence, a positive answer to this initial question acts as a 'gateway' before employees can move onto the next level of engagement. Questions 1 through 6 get you past first base!

Figure 17: Turbo-Charged: An Employee Engagement Model

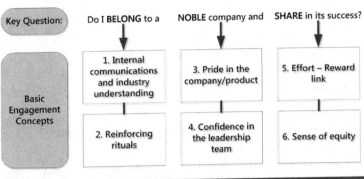

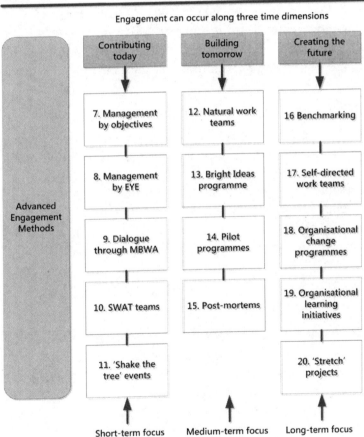

Basic Engagement Concepts

1: **Internal Communications:** Do you have a formal communications plan? Is it first-class? Do all managers adhere to this? How do you know? Have managers received training in communications (presenting, listening, writing)? Is the communications system *tired*? Does it allow for face-to-face dialogue between the senior team and the shop-floor?

   Outcome: I understand what is happening and have the information to do my job.

   Industry Understanding: Which competitors do we admire and why? Which do we not want to emulate? What is the level of competitive threat? Is the reality of the external marketplace really understood? (or is the management team seen to be 'crying wolf'). Are there novel ways to communicate the strategy? (quiz, games, etc.).

   Outcome: We are (or are becoming) the best in the business.

2: **Reinforcing Rituals:** Am I involved in selecting other people who join? Does being a member of this organisation get recognised? (long-service programmes, articles about best employees in newsletters, 'wall of fame', etc.). When something good happens, is it celebrated? Are there mechanisms for my family to participate in the company? (open days, bring your kid to work, parties with partners, company shop, etc.). Do 'work arrangements' (home, hotel, office) signal trust?

   Outcome: I am part of this tribe and my family supports me working here.

3: **Pride in the Company/Product:** Do we have a stated set of values that are inspirational? Do we live up to these? (or, at least, try to). Do our products add value to the wider community? Do we support community activities/corporate social responsibility? Is this well communicated to staff? Overall, how well do we communicate 'who we are' to employees? Are we seen to have noble aims?

   Outcome: I work for an organisation that stands for something positive (more than profitability).

4: **Confidence in the Leadership Team:** Is the senior team credible? ('walk the talk'). Do they inspire confidence? Have obvious underperformance or capability issues been tackled at this level? Does the management team work hard? Have they earned the respect of staff? (technical competence and moral leadership). Do we measure our managers *vis-á-vis* their 'people impact'?

Outcome: The 'pilots' are in control. I feel secure and proud.

5: **Effort: Reward Link:** Am I paid fairly *vis-á-vis* the market? If I work hard, does it positively impact how much I am paid? Am I rewarded for *bad behaviour?* (high overtime payments for working slower). Is there an opportunity for me to move on to something else if I want to? Is there some financial mechanism for 'a rising tide to lift my boat'? (profit-sharing).

Outcome: I am getting a fair day's pay. When a windfall occurs, I benefit.

6: **Sense of Equity**: Am I fairly paid *vis-á-vis* my family and neighbours who do similar jobs? Am I paid fairly *vis-á-vis* my colleagues? Are the 'differentials' between jobs reasonable? (car policies, etc.). Are there obvious status differentials between people at different levels in the organisation? Do these make sense?

Outcome: My value to the organisation is recognised and I'm paid 'on par'.

Advanced engagement methods occur along three separate time dimensions:

Contributing Today + Building Tomorrow + Creating the Future

Contributing Today

7: **Management by Objectives:** Is my role clear and well-defined? Are my objectives clear and measurable? Have I had a hand in shaping these? Do I get good (honest) feedback? Is the process energising? (or a time-soaking piece of bureaucracy).

Outcome: Fog clearance and continually 'caught doing something right'.

8: **Management by EYE:** Do we have visible 'scorecards' around the organisation? Do I keep these up-to-date? Does anyone pay attention to these? Am I allowed to shine?

Outcome: I have a visible way to communicate progress being made.

9: **Dialogue through MBWA (management by wandering around):** Is there a managerial presence where I work? Do I have a real opportunity to engage with the senior players? Is my manager aware of my career aspirations? If I 'challenge the *status quo*' is the reaction positive? Do I have an opportunity to engage socially with my managers?

Outcome: My opinion matters. You are not socially 'distant' from (superior to) me.

10: **SWAT Teams:** Do we 'send in' specialist teams to quickly overcome key organisation problems? Have these teams been trained? Are the teams crossfunctional? (to ensure differing perspectives are brought to bear). Do we avoid using outside consultants all the time to fix the organisation for us? Is my talent fully used?

Outcome: Let me show you what I can really do.

11: **Shake the Tree Events:** Do we run 'one-off' events to engage staff around particular problems or opportunities? This can be 'fun' – run along the lines of marketing campaigns, for example, October = Bureaucracy Busting Month. Are these events kept 'fresh'?

Outcome: I know that I am needed here because I am continually asked to contribute.

Building Tomorrow

12: **Natural Work Teams:**[58] Is there a system whereby employees can take 'time-out' to review the way they are working and how this

---

[58] Working in teams deals directly with a conundrum in organisational life: "How can you make 'boring' work interesting?" The design of some jobs (example: cash collection at a toll booth) is inherently boring. Some companies address this by allowing people to become involved in the issues that *surround* the core job – for example, shift patterns, overcoming fraud, design of paperwork, etc.

could be improved? Are staff empowered to make changes? Are employees skilled in problem solving and business process re-engineering?

Outcome: Let us improve it.

13: **Bright Ideas Programmes:** Some organisations run various forms of 'suggestion schemes'. Those that work best seem to have a couple of features in common: All suggestions are acknowledged; those that get through must be implementable; employees should be involved during the implementation phase; some form of reward for good ideas; direct feedback for unacceptable ideas with a 'better luck next time' note.

Outcome: I contribute to a wider agenda. I bring my 'prizes' home and demonstrate my worth.

14: **Pilot Programmes:** Do we engage employees in 'pilots' – for example, the 'branch of the future' in banking. Once this is decided, the idea is to 'pollute' the rest of the organisation with the best practice. Works well where the results can be replicated across the organisation.

Outcome: We operate scientifically (experiment and test) before full commitment.

15: **Post-Mortems:** Used at the end of projects/programmes to assess the learning. Usually a 'fixed' series of questions (which may be reviewed/redesigned annually). Led by the project team leader. No blame-game.

Outcome: Better next time (we learn from past success and mistakes). No search for the guilty.

Creating the Future

16: **Benchmarking:** Employees can become engaged around 'beating an external enemy' (which plays to the tribal instinct in most of us). Benchmarking also can be used to 'soften up' resistance to change (for example, a group of shop stewards visiting a highly efficient overseas plant to witness how reduced manning levels can work in practice).

Outcome: We know where we stand *vis-á-vis* the competition. We have an external 'enemy' target.

17: **Self-directed Work Teams:** At the 'high end' of engagement practices, some companies allow huge degrees of autonomy to teams. They allow decisions that historically were in the control of the management team to be decided by employees. The role of the team leader is critical (traditional *supervisors* can find this change difficult). It is possible to move 'towards' this on a graduated basis (does not have to be 'big bang').

Outcome: We 'own' our work problems and do not need to be supervised to perform.

18: **Organisation Change Programmes:** Have you spent enough time in really understanding the 'today' picture/culture? (we understand the size of the hill to be climbed). Have you engaged staff in the 'creation of a better tomorrow' – something that has more emotional appeal than the way you work today? Do you know (organisationally) 'what you want to be when you grow up'? Is the driver for the change programme clearly visible? ('pain-driven' *versus* 'vision-inspired'). Is it believed? Is there real commitment to this at the senior team level? Was there involvement in planning this within (or is it being 'sold' to the workforce?). Is it possible to make the 'tomorrow' picture graphic?

Outcome: A better tomorrow, which we both understand and support.

19: **Organisational Learning Initiatives:** The best managed organisations allow/encourage people to continually 'learn'. Couple of different possibilities under this heading – for example, continuous professional development, self-directed computer-based training, the development of internal libraries, data from external sources (consultants/conferences), sending key people on development (short and long programmes), scenario planning, 'Standing in the Future' exercises, etc.

Outcome: I am continually 'sharpening the saw' and on 'full headlights' (looking outwards).

20: Stretch Projects: These are tasks assigned to an individual that are 'above' the normal job requirements – for example, investigation of a new technology. Can be 100% (or some other proportion) of the role. Often have a personal development dimension in addition to the business impact.

Outcome: I am growing here. I can contribute to my maximum talent level.

Having Fun: While managing change is a serious business, it does not have to be *po-faced*. In fact, introducing an element of fun, even frivolity, can make a change process seem more human and certainly more memorable. Obviously there is an element of judgement here; a zany method that convinces the workforce that the senior team 'should be committed' (to an asylum) is not helpful. However, in my experience, management teams often are far too conservative in this regard. Many times, I have argued in favour of doing something a little 'outside the lines' but the senior team pulled back from the edge, perhaps fearful of looking foolish to the staff. As Neil Simon, the American playwright said: "If no-one ever took risks, Michelangelo would have painted the Sistine floor". Statoil (now trading as Topaz) bought the argument that humorous or dramatic communications are more memorable and we produced the Deck of Cards Strategy Quiz. The Statoil case is a good example of an organisation taking a risk with communicating how a change management programme will work and we had great fun with this.

STATOIL: THE DECK OF CARDS STRATEGY QUIZ

Statoil went through a major change programme – essentially moving from being a petrol retailer to becoming a mini-supermarket – trading under the **Fareplay** *banner. Petrol is a relatively simple commodity. It does not have a 'shelf-life'. It is generally the same price in all outlets and customers largely manage the purchase on a 'self-service' basis. All good news, except for two things. First, the margin on retailing petrol is extremely tight (single percentages) versus, say, the margin on selling sandwiches (40%+). Second, there was a growing trend towards 'convenience shopping'. As Irish people became more affluent, they not only wanted to buy petrol, but also wine and bread, etc. at the same location. If Statoil ignored this trend, the likelihood was that sales of petrol would decline as customers sought out retailers where they could purchase a range of products.*

Moving into the 'mini-supermarket' business was an enormous challenge for Statoil. They needed to retrain hundreds of staff across the network in food retailing – for example, stock rotation, hygiene and customer services. I worked with the company as it went through a complex serious of changes. At one point along the journey, we were looking to communicate a couple of specific changes that were happening at that point. People have a limited 'bandwidth' and can only absorb so much information, so we were searching for a 'fun' way to communicate the key messages. To help communicate the central changes, we developed the 'Deck of Cards' and held an on-line 'quiz' with staff to work through the answers, with prizes being presented to the best teams, etc. While it was a fun and highly energising exercise, more importantly it reinforced the key change messages. A selection of the 'cards' is reproduced here:

Statoil: The Deck of Cards Quiz[59]

ACE	
Our Premium Club has been a great success. Our target is to	
♥ Annihilate the competition	☐
♦ Send out loads of brochures	☐
♣ Get 90,000 new customers	☐
♠ Get Henrick back to Holland	☐

FOUR	
Under K2, each person in Statoil has	
♥ One Manager	☐
♦ Two managers	☐
♣ Three managers, two supervisors and a prescription for Valium	☐
♠ No manager – it is real empowerment!	☐

TWO	
How long does it take the Finance Department to close the books at the end of each month?	
♥ One working day	☐
♦ Forever	☐
♣ One lunar year	☐
♠ Three working days	☐

FIVE	
We are hoping to conduct a review of the IT (laptops, software etc.) requirements for the Area Managers' in	
♥ April 2006	☐
♦ Switzerland	☐
♣ September 2010	☐
♠ Sometime in the future. We'll get back to you on that …	☐

Pseudo-engagement: We covered the point earlier that clarity of the issues facing an organisation creates the necessary personal motivation for change; the future needs to be made as *concrete* as possible. The best way for staff to understand the future is to help shape it. In one multi-national company where we worked, a plastic card with a new mission

---

59   Examples only; original set used a full deck.

statement printed in a heavily-embossed typeface was distributed to all staff. This was given to us as "a great example of staff engagement within the organisation". Such surface efforts to engage staff are destined to fail. Merchandising can be successful, but only as a reinforcement mechanism. It needs to be accompanied by real efforts to involve people in co-creating the future. Shallow end efforts – *engagement light* – do not get people energised and enthused. Engagement is a full contact sport; pseudo-engagement, like the plastic card example outlined above, is normally a recipe for cynicism. The Statoil change programme worked really well precisely because the company used a variety of mechanisms to engage the workforce around real tasks faced. The Deck of Card quiz presented on a stand-alone basis would be flippant and non-productive. The best way to engage staff is to solicit their input in resolving powerful challenges facing the organisation.

CONVINCING: GETTING SOME EARLY WINS ON THE BOARD

The literature on managing change often contains the idea that organisations should go for some 'early wins' during a change programme. Securing highly visible wins quickly 'convinces' the workforce that change is possible. This lowers the level of scepticism and resistance – making the next series of changes easier. So far, no argument. The usual admonition to managers is to choose 'low-hanging fruit' – tackle an easy problem, get it sorted quickly and move on. If you were attending the gym for the first time, it is probably not a good idea to try to bench-press 150 kilos. You start with smaller weights and build up to the 150 kilos (I have this on good authority from friends who actually go to the gym!).

Heavy Lifting: It is possible to address the 'where should we start' question in a different way. What if you could fix the most important problem facing the business? Something that has proven very difficult to change. If this single issue was resolved – would that send a powerful signal to the organisation about the potency of change?

The best cure for negativity from the sidelines is putting a goal in the back of the net; senior teams need to clock up some early scores to prove that it can be done. Whether this is a small first step or a bigger challenge can be decided only on a case-by-case basis. In terms of *small wins versus taking on the big one*, the individual circumstances will dictate the way forward. Let us look at an example when a company did tackle the 'elephant in the room' issue. The *caveat* here is that you need to be sure of the outcome in advance of the *game going live*. A very public failure on your first effort at change is not a good way to burst from the blocks. And how do you ensure success? Well, just as we learned in primary school, doing your homework usually pays dividends. This is what actually happened.

GEORGIA-PACIFIC: TWIN-LEGS PACKAGING EQUIPMENT

Background: *Georgia-Pacific was a paper manufacturing company, operating from a factory in Finglas, Dublin 11. The immediate presenting issue was an industrial relations claim for increased compensation from the workforce and I was asked to help address this. In order to understand how the management team responded to this particular claim, I needed some historical perspective. The background issues are sketched below:*

Established Precedent: *About 10 years prior to the claim, the company bought out a 'job evaluation' system with significant individual payments being made to the operators in the factory. A similar issue had arisen more recently. Employees in one part of the operation made an argument for increased manning levels. After some negotiation, they were paid €3,700 each and moved from grade 'e' to grade 'f' on the pay scale. In this factory, work that became the focus of a protest was discontinued (the more normal arrangement is that staff continue to work as normal*

*until the issues in dispute are processed under a grievance
procedure). This 'history' of paying for change undoubtedly
coloured the thinking of the union members. They had played the
game twice in recent times and the score was SIPTU 2: Georgia-
Pacific 0.*

Pay Freeze: *The company subsequently had hit a difficult patch,
renegotiated the 'house agreement' and implemented a pay freeze
for two years. Part of the negotiations strategy was a threat to
'close the plant' and to move production to another site. The pay
freeze was significant for two reasons. First, it denoted a
growing 'toughness' in the relationship between both parties.
Second, there was a strong sense that the unions wanted to play
'catch-up', making up for what was considered lost ground
during the earlier recessionary period when the business was in
poor shape. When the company introduced new equipment
('twin-legs' packaging) that would significantly improve
productivity, the stage was set for a major confrontation.*

Twin-legs Equipment: *The twin-legs packaging machinery
was part of a major capital investment. The equipment offered
significant productivity benefits over the existing method of
working – both in terms of numerical output and the fact that
one person could operate 'both legs of the machine'. The union
made a claim that (a) either two people would have to 'man' the
machine or (b) the person operating the equipment should be
paid an additional 50% (a fairly typical 'let's split the benefits'
argument). The company refused but did make an offer of 15%,
which was rejected by the union. The '15% solution' itself would
have possibly led to a number of internal problems. First, it
touched on internal relativity issues. In industrial relations,
Person A is often happy on Salary X until they discover that
Person B is on Salary Y – even if the differential is not 'material'.
Second, the mechanism for making it work in practice would
have been both 'messy' and costly (arguments that the company
should pay this differential to people who provided 'cover' on the
machine, for break times etc.). It remains speculation. The union*

rejected the offer and the practicality of the 15% solution was never tested. The issue then remained in 'stalemate' for several years (that is not a typographical error). Both 'legs' of the packaging equipment had never been run simultaneously in the way that the machine was designed to run. The UK-based head office staff had a mantra that they were not going to 'pay for change' (they were not aware of the earlier instances of this at the Irish plant) and the full utilisation of the machine was never achieved.

Third Party: The company mooted the idea of involving a third party (the Irish Productivity Centre) specifically to look at the grading structures and associated issues. The union agreed to this, but would not accept being bound by the outcome in advance (it reserved the right to reject the findings of the IPC). Again, the sense communicated was of a win-lose bargaining relationship and the issue remained in limbo. At this point, I became involved in overall change management planning at the site and the twin-legs packaging issue emerged as part of this. I asked the CEO if I could brainstorm a couple of potential solutions. He agreed and I came up with a range of options detailed below. The fact that the twin-legs issue was ongoing for several years and the company had already conceded on the 'pay for change' principle by offering the 15% meant that this would not be an easy issue to resolve. The company also essentially had conceded on the 'manning' issue by allowing the spare operator to work with the main operator when the machine was running.

Possible Going Forward Solutions[60]

Option # 1: Do Nothing: *One obvious option was to do nothing. Simply continue 'as is' and not respond to the twin-legs equipment or the recent claim submitted.*

Upsides

- *Little company time/involvement. The organisation has 'bigger fish to fry and IR issues are simply a distraction from the strategic agenda.*

Downsides

- *There is a significant productivity gain opportunity which will be lost if the company does not pursue this.*

- *The likelihood of the IR scene remaining 'static' is poor and this may actually worsen (some form of escalated industrial action if this is ignored).*

Option # 2: Concede the Union Claim: *The company could simply 'concede' the current claim by the union.*

Upsides

- *Would allow the company gain the productivity increases associated with the twin-legs packaging machine (it may not be not cost-increasing as the productivity gain would outweigh the cost).*

- *Visible win for the union, which may help to improve the relationship (albeit I do not believe that it would have this result).*

---

[60] The operators were well-paid by industry standards. The base pay rate was at the 90th percentile in the marketplace and shift premium was paid on top of this. With overtime earnings, the operators were making solid earnings, well in line with industry standards. The central question was how well had this been communicated to the workforce? Effective salary management is often related to a company's ability to convince people that they are paid in line with the market (it is an internal marketing exercise). The quality of this internal marketing is often as important as the actual level of salaries paid. In this particular case, Georgia-Pacific was quite poor on this internal marketing issue.

Downsides

- *Real cost of concession may be difficult to calculate – there may be any number of spill on claims (around the company breaking historical differentials, etc.).*

- *May be a 'tough sell' to the UK management team (this specific point applies to a number of the options detailed in this note).*

- *May be seen to be 'rewarding bad behaviour' and reinforcing similar claims in the future.*

Option # 3: Negotiate (Softly): *Work out a negotiated settlement on the specific claim (the historical claim for the twin-legs equipment and the more recent claim for a general pay increase). Possibly offer a 'trade-off' – concede some payment to the union members in return for a number of specific changes in operational practices required at the plant.*

Upsides

- *Would allow the company gain the productively increases associated with the twin-legs packaging machine.*

- *Shows good faith in not having to go to a third party (if you could manage to do this in-house).*

- *Would provide a sense of closure to this issue for both the union and the management team.*

Downsides

- *It concedes on the principle that you are prepared to pay for change (in reality, is this stance dead on the basis that the 15% offer is already on the table?).*

- *Could it make the Irish operation less viable in terms of labour costs?*

Option # 4: Negotiate (Hardball): *Company could take a 'hard line' in relation to the current claims. There are a number of sub-arguments here:*

- *The payment for change issue is covered in the house agreement and in the National Pay Agreements. A specific element in this is the local bargaining clause. Is there an argument that you can now negotiate a list of internal changes retrospectively?*

- *There will be no further investment in the plant until we maximise the resources that we currently have on site. This is key in terms of the long-term impact on the plant. Do the unions and the general workforce really believe that you would follow through on this or is it seen as simply 'crying wolf'?*

- *Transfer some of the production elsewhere (either to a plant in the UK or subcontract this to an outside vendor). Make the threat visible.*

- *A sub-option under this heading is to introduce a negative condition. My understanding is that this is the only packaging line that has this productive capacity (there are five lines in total working each shift across three shifts). One idea might be to introduce the notion that you need to put on some extra capacity (a night-shift that runs over the weekend) in order to make this operation of the Twin-Leg equipment seem more palatable.*

- *Hold off on the payment of the next instalment of the pay agreement.*

Note: *Possibly you need to steel the HQ staff to take this issue to a third party. Rather than seeing this as a failure of the internal negotiations machinery, you would be consciously using this as part of your strategy to gain acceptance.*

Upsides

- *Re-establishes the management team as being in the driving seat (on the assumption that you can pull it off).*

- *Does not concede on this cost-increasing claim.*

Downsides

- *You have to be prepared for the long haul. Given the 'age' and history of this issue, it is unlikely that the unions will concede easily on this point (do not make the threat unless you are prepared to see it through and have the resources and the willpower to really fight the case on this).*

- *The current upgrading of the restroom facilities may be sending a contra signal – that the company is interested in continuing to invest in the site.*

- *It has the potential to provide some short-term disruption to the business. Would this be a disaster? (or worth taking a hit during a short stoppage for a long-term gain).*

Option # 5: Be Creative: *You could concede something to the union in relation to the required changes and 'pay' for this creatively. Two examples:*

- *Offer an improvement to some general condition of employment that would positively impact all employees and put pressure on the specific group to concede (not quite sure exactly what this might be – perhaps something on school fees/costs for children of employees if this was attractive).*

- *Offer a cash payment to a charity of the unions' choice (for example, Barretstown Camp Project or something to do with kids/drugs/old folks in the local area).*

Upsides

- *It might allow the union to save face, while protecting the principle of not paying for change for the company.*

- *Depending on the charity chosen, it may increase support for the company's position within the general workforce (give ammunition to the moderates).*

- *It may have some beneficial external PR benefits within the local community.*

Downsides

- *Cost of doing this.*

- *You need to have a strong union official (both external and internal) to help 'sell' this message internally. Not sure if this is the current situation.*

Option # 6: Change the Rules of the Game: *It might be possible to change the entire basis of the relationship. For example, explore the creation of a partnership-based relationship with the unions. How this might work in practice is not clear to the management team. We could look at a range of the partnership models that have been created elsewhere to explore how some of the more 'advanced' companies have tackled this issue (the introduction of self-managed teams, the possibility of annual hours contracts, etc).*

How Partnership Works: *The company/union often work with an external facilitator, someone who has specific skills in this area and knows the process. The 'early' part of the game is to agree the process/guidelines, allowing the company and the union to agree the key business drivers/issues. Many of the initial meetings are on 'non-IR' issues. Once the joint union/management teams get through this stage, they then move onto a more 'traditional' bargaining stage/negotiations – but on the basis of a win-win (rather than a win-lose) relationship. If you were thinking of physically moving to a new location this might be a useful time to 'change the rules of the game' (in organisation terms, 'birth is easier than reincarnation'!).*[61]

Upsides

- *It has the potential to radically alter the way in which IR is conducted.*

- *It can unleash a lot of productive talent in the workforce.*

---

[61]   Source: Naisbet, J. (1982). *Megatrends,* New York: Warner Books.

Downsides

- *It is a slow process (two to four years for full implementation in an operation of your size). One of the primary issues is the creation of 'trust' and there can be some fall-out with union-orientated people who feel it is a management scam to take control by the back door.*

- *It requires a huge amount of management time and commitment over a sustained period.*

- *A 'well managed' traditional operation beats a 'poorly managed' new style operation hands-down (you have to really believe in this stuff to make it work).*

What Happened? *The twin-legs issue was successfully negotiated, without conceding any additional costs, as part of a wider change programme at the plant. It involved a complex set of negotiations with the workforce and the full-time union official – essentially demonstrating that the plant was in jeopardy if the existing stance continued (a 'push' change strategy using the definitions made earlier). It remains a truism that within the multi-national sector, the real competition often comes from 'sister-sites' within the same company rather than external competitors. In this particular case, a sister-site in the UK (there was some 'bad blood' between the Dublin and the UK site for historical reasons) had come up with the tagline that 'unions dictate the pace in Dublin' and this did not go down well politically at the most senior levels in the company. Armed with this information, the new CEO Richie Broderick (who had brilliant 'connect' skills) was able to convince the unions that 'winning' on the twin-legs issue would be a Pyrrhic victory and put the overall site in jeopardy. His arguments, delivered in a straightforward and non-threatening way, won the day and the unions conceded on the twin-legs packaging issue. The central point here is that the company was prepared to complete an extensive piece of 'homework' before deciding to 'run down the hill' with a new idea. Once it had good data, it was able to come*

> *up with a measured response, which ultimately was successful in*
> *moving the project forward.*

Let's look at an example of the opposite of this, when changes are made too quickly without thought.

WELCOME ABOARD! HOW DO YOU LIKE YOUR NEW BUDDY?

Sometimes, the results of poor internal communications can be unexpected and very funny. I was working with an insurance company (this one definitely has to remain nameless) when the Human Resources group decided to introduce the 'buddy system'. They had received feedback that the induction process (Americans call it 'on-boarding') was not working well. New people joining found the organisation confusing and disorientating.

The buddy system is designed to overcome this. Essentially, an existing employee is delegated to 'mind' the new staff member for a month or so, until they get settled. The practical impact is that new hires are shown around the physical building, are brought to lunch, introduced to other staff members and have an easy reference point for queries to be answered. The HR department, keen to launch the new system quickly, sought *volunteers* to look after a new hire who was joining the following Monday to work in the Claims area. When no one jumped at this opportunity for personal development, one of the female managers in Finance was assigned the task. The finance crew was particularly busy and more than a little annoyed at the short notice. Despite this, the manager took on the job and decided to give it her best shot.

So far, so good. However, the HR staff forgot to tell the incoming employee about the buddy system and how it operates. The new hire was somewhat taken aback by the 'friendliness' of the finance manager, who diligently carried out the role as assigned. After two weeks, he had a word, in confidence, with his own manager about how to deal with a peer manager who was *hitting on him*. Needless to say, there was great embarrassment all round when the story unravelled. You could not make it up!

REINFORCING: COPPERFASTEN THE NEW CULTURE TO ENSURE SUSTAINABILITY

Therapists who work with families experiencing difficulties spend time helping people to 'unlearn', breaking negative patterns of behaviour that they may not be aware of. In the organisation change arena, successful interventions also focus on breaking negative cycles. The key here is to be specific – telling people both what you need them to do and what you want them to give up doing. The 'trick' is to 'catch them doing something right'[62] and to reinforce the new behaviours.

Leading from the Front: To reinforce change, executives sometimes create new *rituals and signals.* These symbolise what is important within the new environment in a more potent way than, say, announcements at team briefings. Rituals like an 'employee of the month' ceremony allow organisations to reinforce behaviours that are in line with the organisation's objectives. Behaviour sends the strongest signals of what an organisation really values and this has to be led from the front by the managers themselves. As the Jesuit writer, John Powell, reminded us: "Sometimes, what you do is ringing so loudly in my ears, I can't hear what you say".[63] It is said that one day a woman came to Gandhi and asked that he tell her child to stop eating sugar. Gandhi replied, "Come back tomorrow". When she asked why, he said, "I cannot tell another to do what I have not done. By tomorrow, I will have stopped eating sugar".

---

[62] Probably the *most quoted* line from Blanchard, K. and Johnson, S. (2000). *The One Minute Manager*, revised edition, New York: Harper.

[63] Powell, J, SJ. (1990). *Why Am I Afraid to Tell You Who I really Am?*, 2nd edition, Chicago: Thomas More Association.

CASE STUDY: STERLING WINTHROP THAILAND

*Virathep Chatsirivaijaikul was the General Manager of a large
pharmaceutical company, Sterling Winthrop, in Thailand.
Virathep was having difficulty communicating the concept of
'Corporate Citizenship' to his Bangkok-based (mostly
salespeople) team. The concept was part of an overall change
process that had come from head office, located in New York,
many thousands of miles from the Thai operations. I was heavily
involved in the 'rollout' of this across a number of countries.
Most of the suggested new changes were understood and
accepted. The group understood the concept of corporate
citizenship intellectually, but were somewhat sceptical about its
practical impact, sensing that this was just another corporate
mantra from the USA and could be ignored. To bring the
concept alive, Virathep (a particularly creative manager) came
up with an idea. Rather than holding the team's annual
celebratory party at a hotel, he organised an outing to a local
orphanage. The trip was voluntary – no forced labour (with the
exception that all of the management team were mandated to
attend). Each staff member was supplied with paint and
protective clothing. In a single day, they transformed the living
spaces within the orphanage and visibly reinforced the
organisation's commitment to corporate citizenship. A simple
idea – but profoundly energising and effective.*

Key Point: A key element in successful change programmes is the
need to reinforce and consolidate the changes made, guarding against
a gradual slide-back to the old way of operating. A lot of change
programmes encourage representational learning (through language)
rather than behavioural learning (through doing). Adults learn by
doing. If there are tensions between what people *say* and what they

continue to *do*, you need to be alert to this and root it out. This is where there can be a useful role for graphics and merchandising materials.

Internal Marketing: Developing key visuals can have a beneficial effect on the successful reinforcement of change for two reasons. First, developing a model of the change process helps to forge agreement among the management team about what is actually going to happen. We have seen earlier that change programmes can encompass a number of different and complex strands – for example, processes, customer services, organisation structures, and reward systems. A powerful graphic emphasises the rationale for change and shows how the various strands are integrated. The graphic itself is often less important than the process of developing the *model* that forces senior teams to have those difficult conversations. Second, while the change journey may be crystal clear in the minds of the managers (who may have been working on this in advance for some months), having a visual is often a useful shorthand method to bring everyone else up to speed. A picture really can paint a thousand words and is a useful part of the process. There are a myriad of ways to show this. Some organisations use cartoons, some build on a metaphor for change (comparing organisation change to a house renovation), some just set out the major steps that are going to happen in a flowchart/timeline.

Working with C&C, the manufacturer of Bulmer's cider and a range of other drinks products, we produced the following model:

Figure 18: Strategic Plan

Future Fit Vision[64]: Improving the way we run the Business
"We cannot become what we need to be by remaining what we are." **Max DePree**

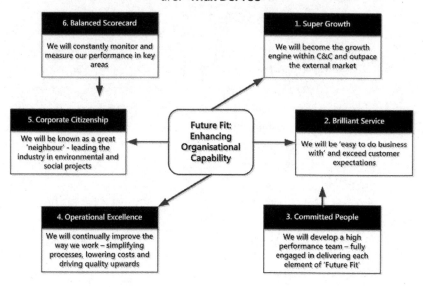

Communicating Company Strategy: One of the most impressive examples of a company communicating its strategy is the Educational Building Society. A summary of what it does is captured below.

❖ ❖ ❖ ❖ ❖

---

[64] This is hardly a 'new' idea: "Where there is no vision, the people perish", *Proverbs* 29:18.

EDUCATIONAL BUILDING SOCIETY

Geography: The EBS has a dedicated 'floor' (16,000 square feet in their HQ building) set aside for this purpose. It could achieve a huge rent for this space but figure that it is a worthwhile investment.[65]

Format: The space is divided into a number of 'rooms'. Similar to the idea in the layout of Japanese garden, each room represents a 'phase' in the organisation's development. The standard of the 'props' is universally first-class — really high-end stuff.

History: There is an entire section devoted to explaining the EBS story (decade by decade). Highlights, lowlights and assets under management (to show the level of growth).

Industry: A full exhibition of what people felt (historically) about the financial services industry (including media pieces on all the big players). This also included negative letters from customers about the EBS.

Strategy: A full outline of the company's strategy took up an entire wall. This was very much along the lines of a 'Strategic Framework' (10 'strands', with solutions projects under each strand, etc.). The wall was magnetised: as progress was made under each heading, projects moved from a red, to amber, to a green magnet. Everything is professionally printed/displayed. When projects get to 'green', there is a 'ceremony' and the team responsible have a celebration.

Strategy Game: There is a huge 'game' painted onto the floor of one room that helps staff to understand how the strategic choices have been made.

Company Values: There is another game/exercise that helps to communicate the company's values and a discussion group

---

[65] Nothing stands still for long in the business world. At the time of writing, EBS is due to move from its headquarters building on Burlington Road, to shared offices in AIB BankCentre.

'seminar room' (with bean-bags to sit on) to work through the issues. A nominated senior executive from EBS conducts these discussions.

Caveat? Perhaps you feel that this is a bit over-the-top, glitzy and marketing-oriented (the CEO *in situ* at the time this was designed had a marketing background). But it was certainly an impressive/innovative communication of a company's strategy, perhaps the best I have ever seen. It was not simply a 'museum', highlighting past glories. It was a living 'project plan' where staff could see how progress was being made against current objectives.

10
CONCLUSIONS

I hope that this book has demonstrated the importance of approaching change management in a systematic way and made the individual steps clear. Successful change projects require a significant commitment of managerial time and emotional energy. That is the downside. The upside is that, properly planned and executed, change management *can* work, brilliantly in some cases. In thinking about tomorrow's marketplace, do you really have a choice? For most organisations, there is no medium-term 'do nothing' option: to stand still is to be left behind.

Complex Process? When change management is 'deconstructed', it can seem a bit complicated – like learning to drive for the first time ("Mirrors, indicator, engage the clutch, move forward slowly. Oh, I've cut out again"). But after driving for some time, it becomes second nature and you do not even have to think about it. Change programmes are similar. After you have been through a couple of cycles, points that seem complex first time out will become semi-automatic. This gets easier as you become more skilled in the process.

Clear Path: A central goal of this book is to encourage practising managers to undertake change projects, using their own resources. A key message was that you do not have to start from a blank page but can learn from the experiences of others. Hopefully, the Transformation Roadmap, alongside the case studies and lessons from other organisations detailed in this book, will have given you the confidence to navigate forward. Even if you don't get it 'technically correct' at every single decision point, committed managers always find a way. You should be guided by the Japanese proverb: "Fall seven times, stand up eight".

The very best of luck on the change journeys that lie ahead.

APPENDIX A
THE TANDEM CONSULTING APPROACH

I hope that you have enjoyed the book and found something useful in the change models listed and the case studies that explored 'change in practice' in real organisation settings. If you would like further information about the *Transformation Roadmap* or details about how we work, visit our website (**www.tandemconsulting.ie**). This note summarises our approach.

Unique Offering: Tandem Consulting offers four key benefits to organisations facing change:

1. **Skilled Team:** Insights from real-life change experiences have shaped our approach. Each Tandem consultant has designed and led successful organisation change projects, learning the lessons from successful and less successful change interventions. Sustainable change happens when attention is invested to both *hard* (structures, processes, measures) and *soft* organisation capabilities (vision, skills, engagement). The Tandem Consulting team has a unique blend of social science and business experience – bringing both lens to bear on client assignments.

    We have worked on a diverse range of projects, including strategy creation, customer service improvements, mergers/acquisitions, employee engagement and reorganisation projects. The depth of consulting talent across the team is brought into play during projects through the use of the 'client case' method adopted from the social sciences arena (at key junctures, we review and comment on the work completed by other Tandem consultants, maximising the impact for your organisation). Tandem Consulting does not employ any junior partners – all of our team are highly experienced in their particular specialism.

2. **Client Partnering:** We work in partnership with clients, focusing on what is working well, alongside what is broken, to deliver *sustainable* change and a legacy of high performance. Our clients

are not passive recipients of service but active partners in the search for improved performance. We empower clients to self-diagnose and jointly search for solutions. Why? Because working *alongside* clients yields powerful transformation results.

Tandem Consulting respects and fully uses the inherent capabilities of the client organisation. Our aim is to equip leaders and teams with the necessary 'thinking and tools' to drive future changes confidently themselves. A key residual value is equipping organisations' leaders with *change-ability*: a toolkit of skills and techniques that remain in place long after the specific project has been completed. We work alongside leaders and teams throughout each key step of the change process. Ideally, we are 'at the table' during the early planning discussions. As each critical phase unfolds, we focus on overcoming obstacles (through executive coaching, facilitation of progress reviews; mediation/conflict resolution; change management skills training for line managers; employee selection and assessment, etc.). In this way, key change skills are delivered on an 'as needed' basis.

3. **À La Carte:** Clients needs are unique and all assignments need to 'custom fit' these requirements. Clients can choose to avail of Tandem's expertise in a combination of ways:

- End-to-end change consulting support and project management.

- Facilitation of key planning, decision-making or review meetings. All too often, dissenting voices and alternatives are overlooked or closed down and we can help you to avoid this.

- Executive coaching or on-the-job coaching with an action-learning focus. Goal = getting managers within your organisation working at full tilt.

- Delivery of specific training workshops (change communication skills for managers, the psychology of transitions, dealing with hostility). Sometimes, the management team knows exactly where they want to go but lack the skills to execute. Short, sharp training interventions can bridge the gap.

- Design of critical change tools (change readiness, training materials, key communication scripts, individual assessment and selection tools).

4. **International Benchmarks:** Tandem Consulting's depth of
   experience provides an insight into industry best practice. Our
   network of client organisations offers high-calibre benchmarking
   data and case studies for comparison. Part of our contract with
   clients is that we use this experience to develop our own practice –
   while fully respecting client confidentiality. Ongoing research and
   process improvement is part of our offering to all clients.

APPENDIX B
SAMPLE INTERVIEW PROTOCOL FOR INITIAL DIAGNOSTIC REVIEWS

With the senior team:

- In terms of the overall operation, what in your view is working really well?
- What makes this company/organisation distinctive or unique?
- If you compare the operation to other plants in the company, how do you 'stack up'?
- If you compare the operation to other plants in the locality, how do you rate?
- What are the 'top three', the really big issues that need to be resolved here?
- Why?
- What has been done to date to try to resolve these issues?
- How would you see these issues being resolved?
- Do you believe any fundamental 'mistakes' were made in the past? (If so, what?)
- Is there anything else you would like to see addressed that we have not touched on?

With individual managers:

- If you compare the operation to others where you have worked previously, how does it 'stack up'?
- What are the 'top three', the really big issues that need to be resolved here?
- Why?
- What has been done to date to try to resolve these issues?

- How would you see these issues being resolved?
- How do you see your personal role in pushing this agenda forward?
- In terms of employee/industrial relations, what in your view is working really well?
- Is there anything else you would like to see addressed that we have not touched on?
- Do you believe that there will be a positive outcome to this process?

With groups of employees:

- Tell me what it is like to work here? What in your view is working really well/is positive about the company?
- What are the 'top three', the really big issues that need to be resolved here?
- Why?
- What has been done to date to try to resolve these issues?
- How would you see these issues being resolved?
- Is there anything else you would like to see addressed that we have not touched on?
- Do you believe that there will be a positive outcome to this process?

APPENDIX C

'FUTURE PROOF': BUILDING A HIGH PERFORMANCE OPERATION – DETAILED CHANGE COMMUNICATIONS FOR STAFF[66]

This document addresses four central issues:

- How changing market and financial conditions are impacting the company.
- An outline of the detailed work changes that we need to make to secure the future of the business in Dublin.
- The redundancy package for staff exiting the business.
- Improvements to conditions of employment for the remaining workforce.

SECTION # 1: THE EXTERNAL MARKETPLACE

Listed below is an overview of some of the major forces that we currently have to contend with. We have gone into some detail to highlight the current trading climate and financial position of the company. This is the actual picture, not some form of pre-negotiations window-dressing or softening-up exercise.

---

[66] *Note:* Sensitive market information has been removed from this document. It demonstrates the amount of information that needs to be given to staff – where major changes are expected from them.

New Competitive Pressures

1. New entrants in the Irish marketplace

The marketplace has become significantly more competitive in the last two years, particularly with the encroachment of Company ABC into the packaging market. Its products have taken X % share of the marketplace over the last 18 months.

During the same period, PrintCo's share of the packaging market reduced from X% to Y%, while our share of the (named) market has marginally increased by 1% (from X% to Y%).

2 We are finding it difficult to compete against 'low cost' imports

Over the last 18 months, we have lost some private label contracts in the economy end of the business because we have been uncompetitive on price. For example, the biggest single packaging contract in the business is DEF. While we have made several attempts to acquire this business (the contract is worth €X+ million annually), we simply cannot compete against the Dutch suppliers as they are significantly undercutting PrintCo on price.

3 Increased competition from local sources

In addition to competing with multinationals (named here), we also compete with local manufacturers. Company GHI in (location named) has redoubled its marketing efforts and are now covering clients countrywide. It is playing the 'Irish card' ('all our products are made in Ireland') successfully, imitating our own selling strategy. It has increased its share of the market over the last year from X% to Y%. In addition, Company JKL in Northern Ireland has increased its capacity with the purchase of a new BOBST machine and is becoming increasingly active south of the border.

The Trend: A lot of packaging manufacturers have clearly targeted the Irish marketplace and only the best competitors will survive.

4 Being 'local' is not enough

To date we have competed with the European and UK companies by being a 'local manufacturer', with the advantage of being able to provide terrific service and quick response to customer needs. Until very recently, our customers have required fast delivery and it has been difficult for foreign suppliers to supply product at the same speed as us. However, the introduction of low cost travel and better shipping has wiped out this competitive advantage. This makes our business vulnerable as our competitive advantage of being a local supplier is lessened.

5 Moving to Euro pricing allowed customers to 'choose on cost'

Euro pricing also has broken down trade barriers and enabled foreign manufacturers to bid for our contracts. All suppliers quote trading prices in Euro and there are no foreign exchange fluctuations. It enables our customers choose the most competitively-priced supplier without taking any risks on currency fluctuations.

Huge Pressures on Price/Cost Reduction

1 Our products are too expensive

Generally, our products are more expensive than our key competitors. For example, we have managed to maintain good margins with key clients because:

- **Single Supplier:** We have a number of 'single supplier' agreements (where our customers do not benchmark us against the marketplace).

- **Value Engineering:** This ongoing programme produces savings for PrintCo and our customer which we divide equally.

Through both of these mechanisms we have managed to keep the plant fully-loaded. However, it does not disguise the fact that our products are fundamentally too expensive.

2 Labour is more expensive in Ireland than other countries

At the moment, €1 of labour cost in Ireland can be purchased for 85 cents in the UK, 78 cents in Northern Ireland and 64 cents in Holland. If the developing countries in Europe (the former Soviet bloc in particular) come on stream, this will put huge downward cost pressures on the business. This declining 'cost/price' issue is one of the factors that explains some of our recent market share losses.

3 Work practices in Europe are significantly different

In our visits to European packaging sites (accompanied by the Irish Congress of Trade Union's personnel), we discovered that manning levels are lower than in Ireland. The companies visited (name them) have superior labour use, which included ...

What Does This Mean for PrintCo?

It's not all bad news ...

On the positive side, we have gained the MNO contract, which was a significant boost. The purchase of our latest packaging machine to replace the one lost in the fire has the potential to give us a significant productivity advantage.

We currently have an excellent reputation with our customers on service and product quality. We need to consider this now — moving towards a position where our customers say: "If you want it done really well, go to PrintCo".

Bottom Line: We can only maintain our position by becoming more efficient and adopting best manufacturing practices to continually improve our cost base. If we do not achieve this, our competitors will increase in strength until they simply roll over us.

Our manufacturing and distribution cost-base must reduce and we must adopt best practices to support the ongoing competitiveness of the business. There is zero sentiment in business. Our customers will only be loyal to PrintCo for as long as we offer high quality, competitively-priced products. If we cannot do this, they will go elsewhere. We are not prepared to allow this to happen.

SECTION # 2: CURRENT FINANCIAL POSITION

In (year), the Irish business is targeted to make a profit of €X. This was on the back of a haemorrhage of losses in (year). We have managed to secure significant reductions in the cost of raw materials and this has led to a return to profitability. However, as you can see from the market data earlier, this turnaround cannot be sustained through price increases.

Repayment of €3 Million Debt

Our parent company PrintCo Corporation has a debt of €X million as a result of purchasing PQR. There are significant restrictions on capital investment as the company needs to generate €X in profits to repay the existing debt as well as to ensure that we have enough money to reinvest for the future. This has a number of implications for us.

The Dublin plant constantly requires investment. However, as we are just one of five sites competing for the same pool of money, our parent company invests in the location that provides the greatest return – the most profitable and secure plant.

We Need to Inject Realism into All Our Expectations

In the preceding pages, you have had access to a 'warts and all' picture about the external marketplace and the internal operating environment. We are very much constrained by the points made. You cannot simply read through the listing of factors and then ignore them.

To restate: The fundamental objective of the management team is to secure the future of this business. We can only do this by operating sensibly. The proposals detailed in this document will allow us to develop a win-win partnership arrangement whereby the company and all of our people can benefits from the suggested changes. It will not be easy but we are committed to working with you to make the necessary changes.

SECTION # 3: FUTURE VISION FOR THE DUBLIN PLANT: KEY PRINCIPLES

The role of the management team is to build a highly successful, profitable operation in Dublin. Our vision is to outperform our competitors in all key areas. In order to secure the future, our plant will become the most competitive operation within PrintCo Corporation and the 'competitor from hell' for other packaging manufacturers. It is not just talk.

We will do this by:

- Growing our market share in 'A' (from X% to Y%) to regain market leadership.

- Growing our market share in 'B' (from X% to Y%) to achieve clear leadership in this category.

- Become the supplier of choice with our top three customers (named here)

How Will We Achieve these Goals?

There are six core 'pillars' to our strategy:

1. **We must provide high quality products.** Quality levels provided over the past number of months have improved significantly, highlighting that it can be done when all of us pull in the same direction.

2. **With exceptional service levels.** Our customers frequently audit our premises, processes and quality procedures against rising quality standards. It is imperative that we meet and exceed

customers' needs at all times. One of our key customers recently commented: "A customer is just someone who hasn't found a better solution yet". We do not need to become paranoid, but we do need to remain vigilant through managing the basics exceptionally well.

3. **Customer loyalty is towards low cost suppliers.** Loyalty is not given to any particular supplier (regardless of how long we have been doing business). Given our cost structure, the only realistic way we can achieve this is through having the slickest manufacturing operation in this industry. We have the capacity within our existing plant to be a low cost supplier. Our labour practices need to match this.

4. **The business must be profitable.** Profits give our shareholders a return on capital invested to date and secure investment for the future. By returning profits to the shareholders, we will develop the opportunity for continued investment in the plant while securing the future for all of us.

5. **Developing a highly flexible committed workforce is the key.** We sincerely believe that the workforce at the Dublin plant is at least on par or better than any workforce at any packaging plant in Ireland. But just having good people is not enough. We need to ensure that our people are fully skilled in all areas of their work. In addition to having the specific skills for the immediate job, we must be flexible in order to meet changing customer needs and standards. We need to collectively *let go* of past management and union 'sins' and come together to develop a better future. 'It has been done that way historically' is not the recipe we need to follow going forward.

6. **Continuous Improvement as a way of life.** This can only be achieved by continuously improving the core business processes. Our goal is to ensure that all employees will be involved in moving the business forward. This will be achieved principally in two ways:

   (a) We will 'up the gas' on two way communications, using team briefings to keep everyone informed of business changes.

   (b) We will set up continuous improvement teams in each area to address problems and opportunities on an ongoing basis – for example, waste reduction, productively improvement, improved cycle times. We will provide these teams with the training, the tools and time to make a real difference.

Our Belief

PrintCo can and will become a place where people are empowered and fully committed to securing the future of the plant. We have now moved beyond the 'thinking' stage and need to convert this into concrete actions that will allow us to tap into the full potential of the workforce. The specific changes required are detailed in the next section.

SECTION # 4: WORK PRACTICE CHANGES REQUIRED

- **Continuous Improvement teams in each area:** We will train all employees in a common approach to solving problems and improving our business processes and practices, by setting up teams to work on specific areas identified for improvement. These Continuous Improvement teams will look at all aspects of the business and will seek to reduce costs, improve service levels, improve quality, improve training etc. Attendance at the training and participation on Continuous Improvement team will be part of the job requirements for all operators.

- **Use of mobile phones:** Mobile telephones may not be used in the warehouse or while using any mechanical handling equipment.

- **Food and drink:** The consumption of food and drink is not permitted in any part of the factory or warehouse other than designated restrooms.

- **Overtime and *Working Time Act*:** Overtime represents a significant cost to PrintCo and it is envisaged that there will be a significant reduction in overtime available to staff in the future. Staff will be asked to commit to overtime when their supervisor requests it and they are then expected to attend as per their commitment. We are committed to fulfilling our business requirements within a 39-hour week. We cannot remain structurally dependent on overtime. At all times, the *Working Time Act* must be complied with and staff cannot work in excess of 48 hours a week. In addition, all staff must have one day off per week. Holidays must be taken within the calendar year and all employees must take at least 10 days holidays together.

- **Pallet labelling:** It is a customer requirement that each pallet of product carries a pallet label. To ensure delivery accuracy, handwritten pallet labels are specified for picked pallets and they should include customer name, pick slip number and pallet number. The last pallet picked for each customer should say 'last pallet'. It is the intention of PrintCo to supply computer-generated pallet labels in the future and it is required that the warehouse staff use this equipment and ensure each picked pallet, slave pallet or full pallet is labelled before loading.

- **Clean-as-you-go:** The warehouse must operate in accordance with the company's *Clean As You Go* policy. For example, each warehouse person must clean up damaged cases and debris on the floor as they go about their warehouse duties. Respect for fellow employees, product, equipment and facilities must be demonstrated. The principle is that the warehouse is maintained to the highest standards at all times.

- **Reporting mechanism:** Any damage to equipment, racking or the warehouse must be reported to the supervisor by each warehouse operative on a 'no blame' basis. It is required that daily mechanical handling equipment check-sheets are completed at the start of each shift by each operative.

- **Night-shift:** In order to smooth the workload and deliver a better level of service to customers, it is planned to use a three-shift system in distribution. This effectively means a permanent night shift of three people. It is required that one of these staff fills the job of Chargehand.

- **Stock record accuracy (SRA):** Ensuring high quality product and stock record accuracy (SRA) is a major problem for PrintCo. Poor accuracy costs money and affects customer service levels. PrintCo is investing in scanning technology both for stock being received from the factory and for picking and despatching stock. It is required that warehouse staff participate in these developments and use the scanning equipment to its full capability. All stock movements in cases, layers or pallets must be recorded on paperwork provided by the supervisors and counted in the manner specified by the supervisor.

- **Transfer of staff:** Employees will be reallocated to alternative work as requested by their supervisor.

- **Manning levels:** Current manning levels are printer #1 day-shift, 11; printer #2 day-shift, 5; helper day-shift, 18; to new levels of printer #1 day-shift, 9; printer #2 day-shift, 3; helper day-shift, 14.

- **Going forward:** Ongoing co-operation with Continuous Improvement: We cannot envisage all of the changes that will be required as the operation moves forward. To support the continued flexibility of the operation, it is imperative that all employees are committed to Continuous Improvement within the plant.

APPENDIX D:
EMPLOYEE ENGAGEMENT SURVEY[67]

INSTRUMENT DESIGN[68]

This employee engagement survey has been designed to help assess the level of engagement of employees in your organisation. If you answer every question, it should take 10 to 15 minutes to complete the survey.

Please be honest. We are interested in your personal views and ideas in order to create a picture of the different aspects of engagement as you see

---

67 Working with a very talented internal team in the National College of Ireland, I developed the original version of this survey method and I have since modified the instrument for use in a variety of organisational settings.

68 The questionnaire can be tailored to suit an organisation if required.

it. There are no right or wrong answers. Free format boxes are included at the end of each section. You can use these to express additional views or opinions or to make suggestions for improvements.

Confidential Survey

We have taken all steps necessary to make sure that your data is kept anonymous and confidential.[69] Completed questionnaires will be returned to Tandem Consulting where the responses will be collated. Only aggregated results will be made available to management to guarantee that your individual responses are confidential. Thank you for completing this survey.

THE KEY FACTORS IN EMPLOYEE ENGAGEMENT

The concept of staff engagement is multi-factored. There are 10 key components to this – each of which contributes to employee engagement. The key factors are outlined below:

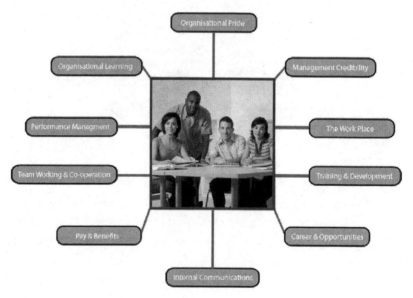

---

[69]   All data will be held in compliance with the *Data Protection Acts 1988 – 2003*. The data gathered will be used in connection with this survey only.

STATISTICAL DATA

1. In which area do you work?

2. Do you work: Full-time? ☐ Part-time? ☐

3. How long have you been working for the organisation?

Less than 1 year   ☐
1 to 5 years   ☐
6 to 15 years   ☐
More than 15 years   ☐

4. How old are you?

Less than 25   ☐

25 to 40   ☐

41 to 55   ☐

Over 55   ☐

5. Are you: Male? ☐ Female? ☐

		Strongly Disagree	Disagree	Slightly Disagree	Slightly Agree	Agree	Strongly Agree
1	**ORGANISATIONAL PRIDE**						
1.1	The organisational strategy is clear						
1.2	I agree with the organisation's strategy						
1.3	This organisation is doing valuable work						
1.4	I feel proud to tell people I work here						
1.5	This organisation makes a positive impact on the community						
	Other comments/suggestions ...						
2	**MANAGEMENT CREDIBILITY**						
2.1	The senior management team is highly competent in doing its job						
2.2	My immediate manager is competent in doing his/her job						
2.3	Promises made by the management team are delivered on						
2.4	The management team operates with personal integrity						
2.5	My manager treats me with dignity and respect						
2.6	There will be follow up action taken on the results of this survey						
	Other comments/suggestions ...						

3	THE WORKPLACE						
3.1	I understand how my work contributes to the organisation's success						
3.2	I have the resources and supports I need for my job						
3.3	I have scope to put a personal 'stamp' on what I do						
3.4	My job is challenging						
3.5	My work allows me to develop my skills and knowledge						
3.6	Health, safety and employee wellbeing are taken seriously in this organisation						
3.7	The 'Green Agenda'/environment is taken seriously in this organisation						
	Other comments/suggestions ...						
4	TRAINING & DEVELOPMENT						
4.1	I have received the appropriate training to do my job						
4.2	I get support and help when I need it						
4.3	My manager actively supports my development						
4.4	I regularly assess my own training and development needs						
4.5	My manager regularly assesses my training and development needs						
4.6	My training and development needs are discussed with my manager						
4.7	I have learned new skills in the last 12 months						
	Other comments/suggestions ...						
5	CAREER & OPPORTUNITY						
5.1	I have good opportunities for promotion in this organisation						
5.2	People are promoted on their ability and experience						
5.3	I see myself working here for the next two years or more						
5.4	Selection for promotion is open and fair						
	Other comments/suggestions ...						
6	INTERNAL COMMUNICATIONS						
6.1	There is a two way flow of communications between management and employees						

6.2	Information is shared regularly between management and employees							
6.3	Ideas on making this organisation better are actively elicited from staff							
6.4	I am able to 'speak up' if something bothers me							
6.5	The culture in this organisation encourages respect for diversity							
6.6	My manager listens to and values contributions from staff							
	Other comments/suggestions ...							
7	**PAY & BENEFITS**							
7.1	Compared with similar jobs in other organisations, I am paid fairly							
7.2	Compared with other jobs in this organisation, I am paid fairly							
7.3	I am satisfied with my benefits							
7.4	I am satisfied with my terms and conditions							
7.5	I currently have good work life balance							
	Other comments/suggestions ...							
8	**TEAM-WORKING & CO-OPERATION**							
8.1	Team members help each other							
8.2	There is good collaboration across the organisation (between functions/departments)							
8.3	There is someone at work I can trust and confide in							
8.4	Team members can discuss issues without it causing conflict							
8.5	Team members treat each other with respect and dignity							
	Other comments/suggestions ...							
9	**PERFORMANCE MANAGEMENT**							
9.1	I receive feedback on my performance on a regular basis							
9.2	Feedback I receive is fair and helpful							
9.3	I am clear on exactly what I am required to do (written goals/objectives and measures)							
9.4	I have sufficient formal opportunities to discuss my performance with my manager							

9.5	My manager notices and values the contribution I make							
9.6	The Performance Management tool used in this organisation is effective							
	Other comments/suggestions ...							
10	**ORGANISATIONAL LEARNING**							
10.1	We continually improve the way we do things							
10.2	It is okay to make an 'honest mistake' here							
10.3	Success is acknowledged in this organisation							
10.4	In this organisation we learn from our achievements and mistakes							
10.5	New ideas and ways of doing things are welcome							
10.6	Individuals regularly contribute new ideas							
	Other comments/suggestions ...							

APPENDIX E

TURNING CRISIS INTO OPPORTUNITY – LESSONS IN CHANGE MANAGEMENT AT LUCENT TECHNOLOGIES[70]

A 'Hard Read' Ahead: In a relatively short period (1998 to 2000), a remarkable sequence of changes occurred in Lucent Technologies. It was a period of confusion and complexity, which I have attempted to capture in this case, based on interviews conducted with the key players. This level of complexity needs to be embraced by the reader in order to truly understand the environment in which executives in these fast moving industries work.

CASE SUMMARY

Lesson #1: Managing Change = Agile Responding

First, the case demonstrates the reality of managing change in the technology sector. The historical notion is that change is a centrally planned and executed strategy in which the outcomes are measurable. The reality, as shown here, may be somewhat different. Effective change management can be conceived as 'agile responding' to circumstances as they rapidly present. This case details a 'white water' turbulent period in which skill in change management was not demonstrated through central planning but through an ability to realign the organisation at lightning speed. Adjusting to changed circumstances is a central skill. It is often said that Internet time is compressed — three months being the equivalent of a year in 'traditional' industries; this case gives substance to this view. The

---

[70] While this case is now a couple of years old, it remains a brilliant example of responding to wave after wave of changes. Dealing with 'continuous change' is often the norm faced by executive teams, particularly in the high-tech sector. This is the story of how one company coped with it.

Corinthians said: "If the trumpet makes an uncertain sound, who will prepare themselves for the battle?". One of the managerial competencies demonstrated in this case was an ability to lead large numbers of people through a very uncertain time period.

Lesson # 2: Driving through 'fog'. Coping with high levels of ambiguity

A sub-point under this heading is the need for senior executives to be able to cope with high levels of ambiguity — and still function effectively. Drucker's comment that "managers are the engine of a business" could have been coined for this team. In order to survive in this environment, managerial intelligence and agility were needed in abundance. But beyond having the 'smarts' to do the job, this team needed a personal ability to cope with uncertainty. It is an ability that is continually tested by companies moving into new, uncharted waters.

Lesson # 3: Prowess in Structuring is a key Competitive Weapon

In any listing of 'factors explaining success', organisational structure seldom features prominently. However, the importance of structure in relation to organisational performance is very much underrated. Where short product life cycles are a feature of an industry, the organisation itself is often in constant turmoil. The ultimate competitive weapon, therefore, is not a particular product-market position, but the organisation's capacity to respond to change (Rosabeth Moss-Kanter, 1993). This 'capacity to respond' is essentially an organisational ability to re-group and restructure, to continually address the 'new game'. The varying 'structural' devices employed in this case (outsourcing chunks of manufacturing, the rapid deployment of project teams, etc.) demonstrate a high degree of competence in using structure as a competitive weapon. Structure provides the 'landing gear', helping to 'ground' change projects and produce real performance improvements.

Lesson #4: Set Big Goals. Then watch what happens.

The case is testimony to the spectacular level of organisational achievement that is possible when a senior team set ambitious goals. It underpins the notion of strategy as 'stretch' rather than 'fit' with existing resources. In reality, the motive for the original change from Stratus to Ascend Communications was more 'pain-driven' than 'vision-inspired'. However, the executive team responded by putting huge energy into the new scenario. It was less 'who moved my cheese' and more 'forget cheese;

hunt for caviar'. The initial skill in responding to external changes progressed to a view that the team should begin to actively seek new business opportunities. The growing confidence of the executive team and their ambition to establish Dublin as a key node in Lucent's worldwide operation partly explains the excellent performance and the increasing sophistication of the Dublin site.

Lesson #5: The Scaleable Organisation: A preview of the future?

Finally, the case highlights the emergence of a powerful new business model — what might be termed a 'scalable organisation'. Outsourcing manufacturing is, of itself, hardly a new concept. It has its roots in the 'putting out' system, which typified the textile industry in England in the 17th century. However, the comparisons end at this point. 'The scalable organisation' developed by Lucent in Dublin offers the possibility of manufacturing to any level of complexity, any volume, within any quality tolerance at the lowest possible cost— seamlessly. The development of a 'scalable' organisation model, including full integration with outsource partners, offered Lucent tremendous flexibility in relation to future products and services. As the industry continues to evolve, Lucent can use Dublin as a portal to 'outsource' products and services — confident that cost and quality parameters will be met or beaten. The 'scalable network' model developed (see later detailed points) has significant potential to yield productivity and flexibility benefits as companies search for dominance of a sector.

CHRONOLOGY

1978:	Stratus incorporated in USA.
1988:	Dublin manufacturing site commenced operations.
1996:	All Hardware Manufacturing transferred to Dublin.
Oct. 1998:	Stratus purchased by Ascend.
Nov. 1998:	Break-up of Stratus into three component parts.
Nov. 1998:	Benchmark Electronics selected as outsource partner.
July 1999:	Benchmark Electronics establishes 'campus' manufacturing facility.
July 1999:	Ascend Communications purchased by Lucent.
Sept. 1999:	Split of agenda into 'excellence' and 'stretch' components.

IN THE BEGINNING, THERE WAS STRATUS

Stratus Computers Inc. was headquartered in Boston, Mass. The company manufactured and sold 'fault tolerant'[71] telephone switching systems — high quality, technically sophisticated products that guaranteed service reliability.

Three business strands, one proposition: Leadership in 'Reliability'

While Stratus built equipment for different 'customer types', the core-selling proposition for these high-end systems was continuity of service. In the event of a failure in the main system, parallel internal processors would 'kick-in', protecting functionality. This was a unique 'belt and braces' design[72] that allowed customers peace of mind. The Stratus equipment was hardwired to complete a self-diagnosis and to switch to an alternative processor when a problem occurred. When this did happen, the machine would call into the home database automatically, alerting the Stratus engineers. The 'mean time between failure' (MTBF) was an incredible 8,000 hours on each processor — a level of service reliability that was almost unmatched in the industry. It allowed Stratus to position itself at the forefront of technology leadership in this specialised sector.

A domestic analogy may help to make this point clearer. Picture the scene at 10:30 am on a Monday morning. The doorbell rings and you go to answer. A repairman stands outside and says, "I want to put a new relay switch into your cooker". You reply, "There must be some mistake. My cooker is working fine". He answers, "I know, but it is going to break down on Thursday next if we don't repair the relay". Stratus moved this scenario from fiction to fact and commercial customers beat a path to the door to purchase the product.

---

[71]   The product denomination changed over time from 'fault-tolerant' to 'continuous-processing' and eventually to 'mission-critical'. For ease of communication, we use the original name throughout.

[72]   Other companies also offered fault-tolerant equipment — but it was configured differently. Many offered a software solution – software would detect faults in the main system and then 'transfer the load' onto an alternative processor. Within the Stratus equipment, fault-tolerance was hardwired into the basic design, giving a better margin of safety with the machine itself acting proactively to anticipate future performance issues.

You can't get fired for buying a Stratus

In the computer world, the refrain "you can't get fired for buying IBM' held sway for many years. It reflected the general perception of 'Big Blue' as a good bet. Riskier applications existed (for example, moving to the Mac OS) that had upsides like simpler user interface but ...

This 'safety first' purchasing logic applied to Stratus products. The rationale for purchasing fail-safe is not difficult to understand. For example, in the telecommunications business: "If a guest in a hotel picks-up a telephone and does not get a dial tone, it's simply unacceptable" (John Barrett, then HR Director, Lucent Technologies). For senior executives in stock exchanges and for air traffic controllers, the logic of purchasing 'fail-safe' is even more persuasive than the hotel industry. The Stratus selling proposition was security of supply, which guaranteed revenue levels. Products were sold under the tag line 'the five nines' (99.999% security guaranteed). In a world of unpleasant surprises, Stratus sold certainty.

Show me the money: High Reliability = High Cost

In order to achieve this level of guaranteed security, customers were prepared to pay large amounts of money. Stated somewhat more colourfully, one former Stratus Manager asked rhetorically, "Was fault-tolerant mainframes a good business? We got customers' wallets, ripped them open and vacuumed up the money. Yes, I'd say it was a good business". A 'typical' system for a bank cost in excess of US$300K but could rise as high as $2M. This was a huge cost when you consider that some of the larger customers had up to 50 systems in place across their network. In addition to the purchase of the 'box' (hardware and software), the 'service contract' was extremely lucrative also[73] (as the equipment was incredibly reliable, the level of 'service' work that actually needed to be completed was minuscule). One manager described the service side of the business as "a license to print money".

In the same way that no-one wishes their house to burn-down to 'prove' their fire insurance cover works, customers were happy to pay high service contracts rates on equipment that did not breakdown. Like paying a premium for a Volvo car to ensure child safety, Stratus customers were

---

[73] Service contracts represented about 30% of the company's overall revenue (typically, 60% of the customer's costs related to the initial purchase; service contracts represented 30% and spare parts made up the final 10%).

purchasing 'peace of mind'. It was a mutually beneficial relationship. Customers gave Stratus a 'haunch' of dollars; Stratus allowed senior executives in client companies to sleep at night, untroubled by breakdown nightmares. Stratus cleverly defended its product pricing using the 'buy cheap, buy twice' notion. It was certainly an effective strategy. By the mid 1990s, the company was reporting worldwide revenue of US$740M — hardly small change for a 'niche' business.

Don't Renege: A Promise is a Promise!

The strength of the 'Stratus Promise' could be seen most clearly in the negative – the customer reaction when occasionally a system did breakdown. And breakdowns did occur. Even the most tightly controlled industries (for example, nuclear power and civil aviation) suffer setbacks and equipment failure. The 'five nines' promise did not guarantee 100% certainty — albeit some customers interpreted it that way.

When the mainframe providing support to the Bombay Stock Exchange shut down, the client, in the words of one manager who was intimately involved, "went nuts". A seasoned manager was dispatched from Ireland, not so much to 'fix' the technical problem (which was sorted in a couple of hours over the telephone) but as a visible apology for the *broken promise*. The manager involved arrived home suitably chastened, describing it as the toughest experience he had ever been through. He'd little tolerance for the humorous quip, "How did you enjoy your holiday in India?", which soon did the rounds of the plant. Bottom line: you don't renege on a $1m+ promise with impunity. Everyone in Stratus knew this; huge efforts were made to build quality 'into' the machines and in responding to service issues when these did occur occasionally.

STRATUS 'PITCHES A TENT' IN IRELAND

In 1988, the company established a manufacturing operation in Dublin. This was part of a planned expansion strategy to establish a global manufacturing and product service footprint. It was also designed to take advantage of the business and taxation advantages of locating in Ireland. As the business grew, the Irish operation expanded. By the mid-1990s, 350 people were employed at the Stratus plant, located in Blanchardstown Industrial Park, a custom-built manufacturing facility eight miles west of Dublin city.

Quick History Lesson: Fault Tolerant Mainframes were intricate, complex products to produce

Fault-tolerant mainframes (FTMFs) had been around in various guises since the 1960s. In terms of 'speed of development', the business was closer to the incremental improvement more often associated with car manufacturing – rather than the frenetic pace and constant breakthroughs within the PC industry. Stratus was effectively sheltered from the storm of 'Moore's Law'[74] and the rapid pace of change in consumer electronics. Yet, while the speed of change in the industry may not have been 'lightening fast', it was an intricate, complex product to produce.

A multi-component product that had been around for almost 20 years posed several manufacturing challenges. Some components were at their natural 'end of life' and new components had to be incorporated continually (and huge quantities of 'old' stock had to be stored as an insurance against future shortages). The intricacies of the product (and the mix of both 'old' and 'new' technologies) posed a challenge around retaining staff who had a *track record* with this equipment. When a system did occasionally breakdown, faultfinding was a mixture of science and experience. Normally two parallel teams, with four to seven engineers in each group, worked on both sides of the Atlantic trying to resolve the issue. They addressed two central questions: Why did the failure occur? and How can we prevent it happening again in the future? Given the complexity of the equipment, it could take up to 16 weeks to resolve a particular query. Newer graduates found it difficult to gain entry to these teams, as elements of the technology was already consigned to 'history' when they had worked through their college curriculum. Labour retention was therefore a key organisational goal.

Dublin takes on all Hardware Manufacturing

Times were good. In the early 1990s, the business was growing solidly and the Irish site was performing well against all the key indices. After almost 10 years in operation, the Dublin workforce had moved up the learning curve, with unmatched quality and productivity levels, ahead on almost every scorecard measure of its 'sister' plant in Boston. Based on this level of performance, the decision was made for Dublin to take over all

---

[74] Processing speed roughly doubles every 18 months. Named after Gordon Moore, one of the founders of Intel.

manufacturing responsibility for the organisation. The Irish star was riding high in the Stratus firmament.

While 'sole sourcing' is unusual in the multi-national sector, the scale of the Stratus business partly dictated this. Economies of scale in manufacturing could be achieved at a single site rather than maintaining two sites on opposite sides of the Atlantic. It also reflected the level of comfort that the US group felt with the Irish plant performance and, in particular, with the Managing Director Eoin O'Driscoll and the extended management team. However, *manufacturing excellence* did not fully account for the success of the Irish operation. A key invisible competence was an ability to 'turbo-charge' the workforce, engaging their commitment and engendering loyalty and performance levels that were atypical in the 'grey' world of computer manufacturing. In the Dublin plant, the local management team had somehow created a 'tribe'.

Moving from a Team to a Tribe: Employee Branding

"We had loads of t-shirts and sweaters with the company logo. People wore them with pride. It was really strange but everyone seemed to 'belong' to the company" said a former Stratus shopfloor employee. The notion of 'employer branding' as a recruitment/retention tactic is of fairly recent vintage. It represents individual companies' efforts to differentiate themselves from the mass of employers, all 'baying for talent' in an overcrowded marketplace. In the mid-1980s, the situation was somewhat different. Unemployment for the decade in Ireland averaged 245,000 people — circa 14% of the workforce.[75] Those who were in a good job felt lucky; the Stratus employees felt luckier than most. Stratus managed to differentiate itself as an organisation in the way it managed its people. The company was superbly 'branded' in the minds of employees. To this day 'ex-Stratus people' still identify strongly with the company. How did they do it? While there is no simple answer, it was achieved through a clever combination of 'hard' (clear goals and good performance measurement systems) and 'soft' ('engaging the soul') human resource management practices. As in many success stories, the genius was in the details: "In most companies when an employee had a new baby, people would say

---

[75]   This point on the unemployment level does not detract from the Stratus success in maintaining top talent. Regardless of recession, there are always opportunities for the better players to move on. During its 10-year lifetime, Stratus lost very few senior managers.

'hey, we are chipping in £5 per head'. In Stratus we brought them in, baby'n'all, to the canteen. We had on-site baby showers. It was more than a company to me; it was family", according to a former Stratus employee, the mother of two children who were born during his period.

Undoubtedly, the relatively small size of the organisation also played its part. As one manager remarked: "It was small enough to put your arms around but large enough to be interesting".

Organisations are the 'Shadow of their Leader'

Stratus was founded by Bill Foster. Born in California, Foster was an engineer who divided his time between business and 'surfing' (the sea — not the net). A 'larger than life' character, Foster founded the Stratus business in New England, which was itself unusual (stereotypically, Americans migrate from east to west—not the reverse). Businesswise, the timing was excellent. Early computers were notoriously fickle. Entering the fault-tolerant business, Stratus 'rode the wave' of companies looking for a solution to the reliability issue. Amazingly, the first Stratus machine was sold to a dairy in Boston; soon the clients became more prestigious as more and more companies looked to copperfasten service promises to their own customers. If an organisation is a 'shadow' of its founder, Stratus certainly reflected Foster's influence. His laid-back, people-first style became a touchstone for the way Stratus managed its people. Foster 'walked the talk' and role-modelled this style throughout the organisation.

Iceberg ahead: The changing competitive landscape

By the end of the 1990s, Stratus had soldiered successfully for 18 years in the USA and for 10 productive years at the Dublin site in Ireland. However, while the company was extremely profitable and had an enviable reputation for human resource practices, there were dark clouds on the horizon. Over the previous number of years, the core-selling proposition had come under attack from two different sources. Firstly, the general reliability of computers had increased enormously. Those of us who are middle-aged remember when the earliest computers were maintained in special, 'clean room' environments — like chronically-ill patients under intensive care in a hospital ward. The second generation of computers became much smaller and more robust; in layman's terms, they simply did not 'crash' as often. Second, the advent of much cheaper 'server' technology offered reliability to customers at a much lower cost. For example, two linked 'servers' offered similar levels of reliability to a mainframe at a cost of approximately $120K — a big discount on the Stratus entry level of $300K. These issues put enormous pressure on the pricing and historical margins enjoyed by Stratus. The competitive waters were heating up. The question was whether this particular frog was about to be boiled!

The market understood and had been tracking these trends. Server substitution and lower price options were reflected in a falling stock price. At the crest of the wave, *circa* mid 1990s, Stratus stock sold for US$40+. Four years later, it was trailing at $15.25. In July 1998, the unthinkable happened: Stratus reported its first loss — $10m. The reasons for the poor performance were listed at the time as the Asian economic crisis, a dramatic reduction in NEC revenues (a key client), Intel's announcement that the Merced chips would ship late and weaker than anticipated business in North America. While all of these were real issues, they masked a more fundamental problem for this business. Orders for FTMFs simply were not coming in. Customers had begun to explore and buy the alternatives. The $10 million reported loss was an ominous forewarning of things to come.

THE END OF THE BEGINNING OR THE BEGINNING OF THE END?

While the falling stock price was a market reaction to the negative industry trends detailed above, it also reflected a view that the Stratus culture was 'soft' on employee relations. Undoubtedly, the company was generous to employees; one vignette neatly illustrates this point. Within Stratus, stock options granted were reissued twice, at lower $ levels, to reflect the fact that the external price had fallen. While this is not 'unheard of', it is unusual. For the external analysts, it confirmed a suspicion that the company would not undertake the necessary organisation surgery required to stay afloat in an increasingly competitive marketplace. Aware of the market sentiment (and acutely aware of the performance tailspin), the company set about tackling the internal mindset that had become 'flabby' on costs. In August 1998, a Reduction in Workforce (RIF) was announced with a goal to cut expenses by 10%. A full-scale project plan was put in place to support this, including detailed communications briefings and the engagement of Drake, Beam and Morin — the premier outplacement consultancy in the USA to help the group affected. Even in cost-cutting, Stratus wanted to "do the right thing" for employees (Pat

Brady, Financial Director). A later strategy-planning meeting at Gemini Peak Ski Resort in Mass., held in May 1998, was to be prophetic. Entitled 'The Beginning of the Future', it would later be labelled as the 'Beginning of the End'. Unknown to the senior executives present at that meeting, Ascend Communications had put Stratus firmly in its sights.

The Pain of Parting: Breaking the News to Staff

Pat Brady, Financial Director, scanned the first-floor conference room. The Stratus senior executive team were seated around an oval table. Outside, the weather was wet and grey—mirroring perfectly the mood inside the room. A collective silence had settled. Just minutes earlier, after months of speculation, Eoin O'Driscoll had confirmed that the company had been bought by Ascend Communications. It was a done deal. No white knights in sight, no going back. The pain in the room was palpable. Mike Devane, head of Manufacturing, always pragmatic, wanted to get a handle on where Ireland figured on the totem pole in Ascend. He argued that the best route forward was to do a 'superb day job' and the rest would take care of itself. John Barrett, HR Director, wondered aloud if they could keep the employee voltage high during the transition; inwardly, he knew from experience that a collective depression would soon settle on the plant. Years of work in climate-building would potentially be blown away. Eoin O'Driscoll, unusually quiet, seemed genuinely saddened at the news. He thought of the organisation, built from nothing with so much passion. Now it was moving out of his control— like a loved child going into uncaring hands. Pat Brady listened to the various contributions. A couple of years older than the other managers in the room, he had lived through three previous take-overs and knew that there was always a 'next chapter'; this book was not concluded. It was too early to tell if it would be a sad or a happy ending. The executive team began to work on the task at hand; planning the communication about the Ascent take-over to the workforce.

BARBARIANS AT THE GATE: THE ASCENT OF ASCEND COMMUNICATIONS

"The day I heard that we were being 'bought out' was probably the saddest day of my career. I know it sounds overly dramatic, but I really loved that company" (former Stratus manager).

In October 1998, Ascend Communications purchased Stratus for US$900m, a US$350m premium on the book value.[76] For the money, Ascend got 2,400 highly-skilled employees and operations in the USA and Ireland.[77] However the real prize was access to a key customer group — the Internet service providers (ISPs). By 'bolting on' Stratus products to its own offerings, Ascend could offer customers a 'one-stop-shop' – consolidating its position in an industry with phenomenal growth projections. While shareholders welcomed the $350m 'bonus' — the Stratus employees greeted the take-over with absolute dismay. Headquartered in Alameda, California, Ascend Communications had a reputation for being 'lean and mean'. In 1998, the company celebrated its 10th birthday. In its relatively short lifetime, Ascend had experienced phenomenal growth through a number of strategic acquisitions. These acquisitions had been 'ridden hard', maximising the economic value. Stratus was 'East Coast, button-down'; Ascent was 'west-coast, knuckle-down'. More than the dress code had changed — and not for the better from the perspective of the incumbent managers.

Overcoming 'Opportunity Lost': The Benefits of Focus

As part of any clinical cost: benefit evaluation, economists use the concept of 'opportunity cost'. This represents the theoretical income lost if the time involved was spent productively elsewhere. The senior team in Ascend were acutely aware of 'opportunity cost'. From an early stage, it became apparent that they did not wish to become embroiled in non-core businesses or ancillary activity. If focus was an Olympic event, Ascend were gold medallists. Jim Heinmarsh, Vice President of Operations at Ascend and the senior USA executive responsible for the integration bluntly stated: "My job is to organise the Stratus acquisition in order that it does not 'eat up' every available waking moment of our time".

A central element of the Ascend culture was to allow autonomy to subsidiary companies. Wide degrees of freedom were reflected in a

---

[76]   At the time of purchase, Stratus held US$400m in cash and US$150m assets: US$550 in total.

[77]   The Irish Industrial Development Authority had been in discussions with Ascend for some time about establishing a manufacturing presence in Ireland. The purchase of Stratus gave the company an instant presence, including a 'ready-made' business model with all the taxation advantages of operating from Ireland.

'hands-off' management style. In Ascend, granting autonomy was not so much a philosophical stance; more an outgrowth of the company's particular history. The company had grown largely through acquisitions — many times moving into 'new areas'. In reality, the senior executive team did not have a particular appetite for the technical 'details' of many of the new business arenas entered —preferring to leave them to the people who knew the business. When questioned about new products in development, one senior executive replied: "I don't spend too much time on the 'stuff' we make". A former Stratus manager (who had great affinity with the FTMFs) remarked disparagingly, "They could have been selling watermelons". The Ascend culture was labelled as 'peel to core'. The positive spin on this is that the management was interested in peeling back all surplus activity, focusing on where the HQ staff could add real value. Viewed more cynically, senior executives in Ascend were focused on building the core business so that they could subsequently sell it to the highest bidder.[78] This was a company working on dipped headlights. The Japanese organisation's concept of a 250-year long-range plan was not on its current reading list.

Crystal-gazing: Rolling back the future

A key unanswered question concerned future business volumes. While the existing business volumes were crystal clear, how would this shake out going forward? The Ascend team was convinced that the best growth potential was in the Telecommunications sector. A key attractiveness of focusing on telecommunications was that the company would build on established relationships. 'Stratus Products' could be bolted-on to the existing Ascend offerings — providing a powerful rationale to do business with the company. Properly executed, it would allow Ascend Communications to move beyond its 'boutique' offering, consolidating its presence with this critically-important group of customers. Picture a Sunday morning shopper, looking to purchase a newspaper, a carton of milk and some freshly baked bread. Option A is to go to three specialist stores and buy each item in turn. Option B is to go to one store that sells all three. One stop; one relationship; one bill; no contest!

When Ascend Communications purchased Stratus, business volumes were split 50:50. Telecommunications broadly accounted for half the revenue;

---

[78] For a useful discussion on this, see Beer, M. and Nohria, N. (2000). 'Cracking the Code of Change', *Harvard Business Review*, May/June, pp 133-141.

financial services and 'mission-critical systems' closed-out the remaining volumes. The view in Ascend was there would always be a 'niche market' outside of telecommunications (some customers were prepared pay a high premium for equipment that could insulate them from a business shutdown and also had a historical affinity for Stratus products). However, given Ascend's focus on servicing ISPs, the key question was: "How can we exploit the business opportunities that lie outside of telecommunications?" A 'call' had to be made on banking and mission-critical applications. Should they be 'sold off' or given a new *home* within the Ascend family? Complicating this decision, there were a number of contract issues that needed to be resolved. Customers who had made huge capital investments purchasing FTMFs from Stratus were unlikely to 'roll over' if Ascend decided to 'walk' from its contractual responsibilities. This risk needed to be incorporated in any solution chosen.

It's quite complex: Why don't you figure it out!

After 'running the ruler' over the strategic options without any immediate obvious answer, the seeds of an idea began to slowly ferment in the US. Why not let the senior team in Ireland 'go figure?' In a memorable piece of understatement, Jim Heinmarsh, Vice President of Operations at Ascend stated, "I'm busy, you four guys will just have to fix that for me". The basic plan would be decided by the Irish executive team — with final approval vested in the US. The Irish management team had a solid 'track record' within Stratus – this trust level had been earned. It also reflected the business reality for the Ascend executive team in the US, struggling to cope with the complexity of managing a new acquisition — side-by-side with major ongoing acquisition activity.

The Good news is you are empowered: Bad news = don't screw up

While this may seem like a textbook example of trust and empowerment, there was a darker side to the Ascend culture. Where people did not measure up, the company could be 'brutal'; these managers took up the challenge knowing that they had to perform or leave. The Ascend culture was 'fault intolerant'; there would be no appetite for excuses. The executive team in Dublin was faced with managing a range of strategic issues, some of which were contradictory:

- How can we maximise the value from the core business relationships? (Servicing telecommunications clients)

- How should we manage residual responsibilities? (How can we minimise potential service liabilities from existing customers whom we now 'own'?)

- How can we establish the 'ancillary businesses' (building FTMFs for financial services and mission-critical clients) to ensure they do not drain the available management time?

- How can we eliminate headcount and all unnecessary overheads while continuing to keep the climate positive?[79]

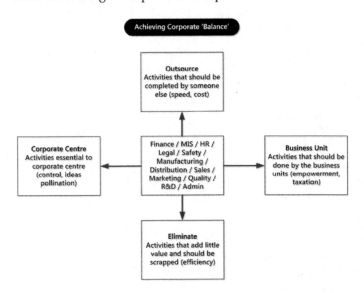

Partly, the thinking was driven by an attempt to achieve 'corporate balance' — deciding what needs to happen at the centre *versus* within the business units (see above).

The solution eventually arrived at was both creative and courageous, justifying the level of trust placed in the Dublin team. In November 1998, following intense internal debate, the company split into three new, separate entities, each with a defined, unique mission.

---

[79] There was little sensitivity in the US to the pain or angst that a full-blown redundancy programme would cause at the Irish operation. While the issues surrounding the impact of this on critical labour retention were understood intellectually, emotionally there was little empathy with the position of the Irish executive team.

From Strategic Thinking to Strategic Implementation

1. Ascend Communications International	2. Stratus NewCo (called Stratus Enterprise)	3. Contract Manufacturing
Service internet service provider networks. 21 of the existing Stratus team moved into this company. An additional seven people were hired bringing the total strength to 28. Seen as the 'most significant' of the three businesses in terms of future growth potential.	Continue to sell FTMFs into financial services and mission-critical applications. New customers were assigned here.	Decision made to outsource all manufacturing of the products. The remainder of the Stratus workforce in Ireland (*circa* 230 employees) would move under this umbrella — move across to some new contract manufacturing company or become redundant.
Goal	**Goal**	**Goal**
Build this business alongside the existing Ascend business in the Telecoms sector. This was seen to have tremendous 'strategic fit'.	Continue to grow the banking and financial services business and 'mission-critical' applications outside of ISPs.	Outsource all manufacturing to a new 'partner' company and maximise 'scale'.

Once the decision had been made to split the Stratus business into three parts, the next question was to decide how to staff these. A critical decision was around the appointment of a General Manager for each business; it was resolved as follows:

- **Eoin O'Driscoll is selected to front Ascend Communications:** Seen as the most important of the three new organisations, a key goal for Ascend Communications was to ensure that the 'crème de la crème' of the executive talent pool were retained in this particular business. With over 1,300 multi-nationals fishing in the same talent pool in Ireland, the better players would have no difficulty in moving to other opportunities. In addition to his managerial skill, O'Driscoll's personal 'connectivity' within the technology sector in Ireland was seen as a significant asset. He was well-known in the marketplace, having run Wang's manufacturing facility in Limerick (800 people) at the tender managerial age of 28. Subsequently, he had stayed in the sector and had built up a volume of tremendously useful contacts. The decision was made that O'Driscoll would head up the Ascend

Communications operation. The logic was simple; if you are going to 'bet the farm', play your best hand.[80]

- **Steve Kiely moves to Stratus NewCo:** Steve Kiely, the VIP of Engineering in Stratus was made President of Stratus NewCo. Kiely was another 'larger than life' character, both physically and intellectually. Always somewhat of a free spirit (or 'maverick' depending on your point of view), he was seen as a perfect 'fit' for this new operation. Kiely was told to set up a new independent business in which Ascend would take a 20% stake, 20% was to be given to staff and 50% sold on to investors. The plan was to take this business through an IPO. It was an interesting gamble, offering several positives. First, it absolved the senior team in the USA from getting involved in 'non-core' activities. Second, it offered the possibility of a high return on the initial investment if the IPO was successful.[81] Finally, this company would also take over existing service contracts (thereby avoiding any potential costly litigation around continuity of service). From the perspective of Ascend, it was a case of heads we win, tails we win.

- **John Killiney[82] takes on contract manufacturing:** John Killiney, former Manufacturing Director in Stratus was put in charge of this

---

[80] I came to know Eoin quite well during this period and, later, when he was on the Governing Body of the National College of Ireland. He has a brilliant strategic mind and the best 'tolerance for ambiguity' of any executive I have ever worked with. I'm probably too old now to start any fan clubs, but Eoin would have been a potential candidate!

[81] While there were some restructuring costs associated with this, these may not have figured prominently on the radar screen. This itself may reflect a cultural difference between Ireland and the USA. One senior finance practitioner's view is that USA companies do not see restructuring costs as material as they are effectively a 'once-off' and not carried forward. US companies were said to be 'prepared to bite the bullet' with regard to restructuring— more so than equivalent Irish companies. In reality, it probably also reflected Ascends strategic goal to 'put its house in order' – before selling on.

[82] The benefit of the GM role for Killiney was threefold. First, he would be elevated to a # 1 slot — albeit in a smaller operation. Second, he had the opportunity to make some serious money. Because of the high income tax regime in Ireland, it is difficult to 'get rich' on salary — almost regardless of the amount paid. Stock options provide a superior alternative as they receive different (read as 'lower') tax treatment. Finally, Killiney had the opportunity to gain autonomy — freedom to manage with a team of people whom he would

project. In 1997, Killiney had won the 'President's Award' for manufacturing excellence in Stratus, which had raised his personal profile in the company. The wheels were set in motion for the establishment of a fully outsourced contract-manufacturing model, which would build FTMFs for all customers. This was a huge 'leap of faith'. Most organisations that go down the contract-manufacturing route put their eggs in a number of different baskets (wing mirrors are made by one supplier; engine mounts by another, etc.). The *mothership* company often maintains the core manufacturing responsibility — pulling the diverse elements together. In manufacturing fault-tolerant equipment, this 'divide' option was not really possible. Given the complexity of the product (and the fact that everything ended up inside a 'single box'), outsourcing was a '100%'—womb to tomb— decision'. For Ascend, the move to contract manufacturing potentially provided an 'aspirin' to solve a giant logistics headache. But, could it be made to work in practice?

From a Control to a Commitment Paradigm

The splitting of Ascend into three separate businesses posed considerable challenges for each of the functional managers (John Barrett in HR; Pat Brady in Finance and Mike Devane in Manufacturing):

	Issues	Solutions
Human Resources	How can we 'outplace' 250 staff without industrial disruption?	Outplacement through natural wastage and huge efforts to help people see Benchmark (see later) as an alternative – but still excellent – place to work.
	How do we maintain the critical talent to run the new business?	Clever financial incentive package that gave the group a 'sense of ownership' of the new businesses without *giving away the store!*

personally select from the remaining Stratus troops. On almost every level, it was a recipe for success.

	Issues	Solutions
Finance	How do we get an external company to agree/gear up for an 'elastic' forecast volume projection?	Developed the concept of a 'phased withdrawal'. In simple terms, this guaranteed the current level of income (to maintain 250 people on the payroll) for 12 months. In year 2, the percentage dropped to 80% and was phased out by the end of year 3.
Manufacturing	Given the complex nature of the technology involved, how can we 'transfer the learning' from Ascend to a contract manufacturer?	Transfer the existing group of people. Ask the successful contract manufacturer to establish a manufacturing 'campus' presence in Dublin to exploit this talent.
	How can we ensure that quality standards are maintained?	Ride shotgun on the output of the new plant—ensuring that quality standards are maintained.

New Paradigm: To 'get' 'control', let it go!

In addition to the complex 'technical' issues posed in each area, it raised a new paradigm: how do we control a process and a group of people with whom we do not have any formal reporting relationship?

What emerged from the (sometimes contentious) debates around this was a questioning of the historical control paradigm — and the emergence of a new realisation. In order to build a healthy, functioning relationship with the outsourced manufacturer, this group would have to 'let go' of their historical control mode. Just as a parent at graduation begins to see their offspring in a new light, the group needed to evolve a new type of relationship with the contract manufacturer— one of genuine partnership. Cutting to the chase, *screwing the contractor* would provide a Pyrrhic victory. John Killiney summarised the eventual deal as follows: "The deal with Ascend gave us the breathing space to build a fully, workable business. It was an act of faith which I like to believe we've since reciprocated".

BEYOND THINKING TO IMPLEMENTATION: MAKING IT HAPPEN

Intellectually, the problem had been cracked. All that was left now was to make it happen. There was no problem with the 'gang of 21', who had been selected to be part of 'Ascend Communications' – the most important going forward piece of the business. Indeed, the letters sent to this group were positive and upbeat—reflecting the notion that they had in some way 'won'. Similarly, the Stratus new company team would feel they had done well in this particular lottery. The main HR problem was in transferring the bulk of staff to some (as yet unknown) contract manufacturer. With the preconceptions about contract manufacturing being the 'lowest form of employment', it would be a tough communications challenge:

"It's difficult to describe how I felt when I was told I had to leave the company and move into a contracting company. At first, I felt let down — I'd always worked hard for Ascend and this seemed like a negative reward for loyalty. I felt excluded; why had I not been chosen to go the new company? Most of all, I was really worried about whether, at 45 years old, I could start all over again" (former Stratus/Ascend employee who eventually went to work with Benchmark).

Call 911: The positive Stratus climate died!

During the changeover, a collective depression descended on the operation. Partly this was driven by insecurities around employment; during a 'reduction in workforce', it is virtually impossible to maintain a positive climate. Ambiguity and insecurity mixed together coalesce into a powerful, negative cocktail. The company needed to 'target' some of the senior technical employees to ensure their skills were retained in the business. At the next organisational level, many of the 'blue-collar' workforce 'would vote with their feet' and move to open positions in the geographical vicinity. The Celtic Tiger, roaring at that time, took care of some of the pain. But some people did not want to make the move and pushed back against the individual selection decisions: "People came to see me in my office, in the pub, called to my house, everywhere. The message was always the same — 'I need to be in Ascend'" (John Barrett).

Without doubt, the game was seen as zero sum —the 'winners' being the group who moved into Ascend with the 'losers' being 'outsourced' to some (as yet unknown) contract manufacturer. It was like playing 'musical chairs' with some of the seats pre-assigned. A number of employees had worked for contract manufacturers previously. Based on this (largely negative) experience, they were reluctant to re-enter a world of 'no gimmes'. Contract manufacturing had 'second cousin' status in Ireland — with connotations of high volume, low cost and tight margins. The ambiguity surrounding the employer was compounded by a plethora of additional issues, uncertainty around security ("Will I have any job?"), conditions ("Will I be able to pay my mortgage?") and location ("Will I be able to stay in Dublin?"). In fog terms, this one was a pea-souper.

Heard it through the Grapevine: stock options news explodes

Fuelling the transition difficulty, the group destined to move into contract manufacturing were in the same office space as the Ascend Communications 'gang of 21'; the perceived 'winners' and 'losers' were sharing workspace. While later, some of the employees would move to a new campus manufacturing facility on the same industrial park, in the interim the two companies lived side-by-side in an uneasy alliance. In large organisations, it is always difficult to keep anything secret – especially 'bombshell' news. Word leaked that the 'chosen 21' had been given substantial stock options by Ascend as an inducement to stay with the company. From Ascend's perspective, it made perfect sense to try to 'lock-in' critical talent but, understandably, not everyone shared this 'company' view. The news rapidly travelled through the grapevine; soon the rumour had festered into fact. There was open revolt by people who felt that they had suffered a triple whammy:

- Not being 'chosen', with the accompanying loss of self-esteem.
- Losing good employment, moving into low status 'contract manufacturing'.
- Missing an opportunity to make some money and financial security.

The human resource strategy (keep as many people as possible) was starting to unravel in a climate described as "absolutely brutal" by a former Stratus employee. Some of the 'contract manufacturing' group had critical skills, not easily replaceable in the short-term. Years of experience in building a complex product, with all the tacit learning which accompanies it, was in danger of being lost.[83] John Barrett was told bluntly by Jim Heinmarsh in the USA: "I want this situation fixed". The eventual solution was to develop a retention deal with the 'top 40' staff who were to transfer to Benchmark. Individual agreements were made with key players

---

[83] For a useful discussion on this, see Morris, T. (2000). 'Promotion Policies and Knowledge Bases in the Professional Services Firm', *Career Frontiers*, Oxford: Oxford University Press.

and post-dated cheques written to give visible evidence. It worked; the turnover of key players abated and the immediate storm was ridden out.

Choose your partner: Key selection criteria

It became ever more important to move on choosing a manufacturing partner. Before this could be done, the available options needed to be sketched out and clinically assessed. The BIG issues can be summarised as follows:

Options	Issues Raised
#1: Outsource the manufacturing of the FTMFs to a third party.	Transfer risks (for example, quality). Costs (for example, need for additional internal people to 'manage' this relationship).
#2: Complete the manufacturing in-house (continuing to use the existing Stratus manufacturing capability).	Affordability (as margins were being squeezed). Low risk was a plus.
#3: Have the manufacturing completed at some alternative location within Ascend.	'Fit' with Ascend business seen as poor. Not a real option.
#4: Sell the business to the existing employees in a management buy-out.	High 'risk' (unproven group).
#5: Sell the business to a third-party company.	Commercially solid. Jettison 'future' growth in this area.

The Ascend view of the world was crystal clear on this. It wanted to 'stay in' the 'fault-tolerant' business, selling FTMFs. However, it wanted to outsource the manufacturing element. Option #1 was the cleanest fit with these objectives.

Contract Manufacturing Beauty Parade

As part of the 'keeping life simple' philosophy, a decision was made that there would only to be one source of supply for the hardware. While 'multi-source suppliers' is the anthem for junior purchasing managers the world over, the complexity of building FTMFs dictated that the company could only 'get into bed' with one partner. The initial courtship would have to be managed clinically well and the eventual commitment made to work solidly.

If the strategy had been to 'end-life' the product, the decision on a contract management partner would have been somewhat easier (predominantly cost-based). However, the ongoing liaison with 'quality fanatical' customers (NEC in Japan was a perfect example), coupled with the likelihood of running the business as an ongoing concern, meant that the 'height of the bar' was raised in choosing a potential partner. All of the major worldwide contract manufacturing players were contacted; those who expressed an interest were sent a detailed 'partner specification'. Following an initial 'whittling down' process, a meeting was held in California with the three 'finalists': Benchmark, Celestica and Selectron. In the interim, a detailed 'selection criteria' checklist had been devised and completed by the senior Dublin team. In practice, the degree of differentiation between the three companies was slight; commercially, there was nothing to choose between the individual bids;[84] it was likely that the final decision would have to be made on something other than commercial criteria alone. Each of the three companies brought particular strengths to the table:

- **Benchmark:** Headquartered in Texas, Benchmark had existing manufacturing facilities in New Hampshire, Oregon and Alabama (US) and in six additional countries. A huge plus for Benchmark was that the company already manufactured complex boards for Stratus and could continue to make these under the new arrangement (the 'transfer of manufacturing' is always problematic).[85] This 'deal' would represent a vertical integration for Benchmark, a route it was keen to pursue. Benchmark's CEO, Don Nigbor, made it clear that the company would establish a presence in Ireland (the company had already looked at some possible sites). On the downside, there were two concerns about Benchmark. First, the company was the smallest of the three

---

[84] Celestica scored 49; Benchmark 51 and Selectron 54; the numbers were not statistically significant.

[85] One possibility, if any of the other contract manufacturers had been chosen, was that they could have continued to purchase the boards from Benchmark. However, this would have been a potential conflict of interest – they would not have any underlying rationale to make the relationship work – and even had some upside if the relationship soured.

possible 'partners'. This was important in relation to managing the human resource element of the change. Would the group who moved across see a possible 'career future' for themselves in a small organisation (or 'vote with their feet' and move on)? Second, Benchmark had just purchased EMD, in Wynona, USA, another board manufacturer. It raised the question of whether it had the managerial bandwidth to cope with this level of change at the same time.

- **Celestica:** With operations in Toronto and Manchester, the Celestica 'business model' would have granted a lot of autonomy to the Irish operation. It positioned itself as 'hands off' and this was seen as an attractive part of the culture — along with the fact that it recognised the importance of managing the people dimension well. However, the chief downside was the level of 'risk averseness' communicated. Celestica was legalistic in approach. The exchange of documents communicated a company, which, in the words of Mike Devane, "wanted a CYA on every contingent possibility. We just couldn't live with this". Celestica wanted a five-year deal with a host of commitments and guarantees. Neither the local management team nor Ascend's lawyers felt comfortable with this and the decision started to move away from Celestica.

- **Selectron:** Based in Milpitas, California, Selectron was a former winner of the Malcolm Baldridge Award, the most prestigious quality award in the USA.[86] Selectron had an existing presence in Ireland that the Ascend business could simply be 'bolted onto'. However, while offering the benefit of 'simplicity', this also posed a potential downside. The Ascend group would become submerged as part of the existing Selectron team. The risk here was that the group would feel like 'small fish in a big pool' and would not be treated with the level of respect that their particular skills demanded. While this never formed an explicit part of the negotiations, this was the strong sense created.

Following the meetings in the USA, each company was invited to come to Dublin. It was difficult to decide on a 'marriage' partner after a single date;

---

[86] Quality is used here in a broad, rather than a narrow, functional sense. It includes product quality, customer service, process improvement, employee engagement, etc.

a second round of meetings in Dublin was booked to allow the parties to explore the relationship further. The rigorous process followed underscored a central belief. In order for the relationship to really work, it needed to make more than just economic sense; it had to work at a 'chemistry' level between the two organisations. The senior team in Dublin were conscious of the number of mergers, acquisition and strategic alliances that fail, not because the original rationale was flawed, but because the 'chemistry between two organisations does not gel. During a 'second cut' of the data, the Dublin team ran the ruler over all three companies using a Human Resource template devised by John Barrett, the HR Director. Using this particular lens, Benchmark became the clear favourite and this data figured prominently in the final decision.

Benchmark Selected: Relationship established on an 'Open-Book' Basis

In January 1999, Benchmark was selected as the partner of choice. Immediately, Benchmark established its first manufacturing presence in Ireland and the complex 'handover' task began. The relationship with Benchmark was agreed on an 'open book' basis. All costs were open to scrutiny – not because Ascent wanted to 'nail' Benchmark on costs – but to allow them to make "the decisions they needed to make" (Mike Devane). Over time, Ascend would 'build-in-controls' (chiefly focused on operational spending and purchasing) but this would happen over a 12 to 15 month period. The initial relationship was built on high trust between former colleagues. "They were our campus supplier. Of course, it was in our interest to make them a success" (Pat Brady, Finance Director).

POST-SCRIPT: THE BENCHMARK SUCCESS STORY

On almost every business index, the Benchmark story was positive. Some examples include:

- In 2000, the Benchmark stock price increased by over 100% over a nine-month period. Many of the employees who joined Benchmark were now stock owners and profited from the move across.
- John Killiney went on to run operations in Sweden, Hungary, and Scotland, along with two plants in Ireland — Dublin and Cork,

with the Dublin site becoming a key part of the Benchmark growth engine.

- The business relationship between Ascend and Benchmark was extremely positive. While no business relationship is perfect, the issues that typically arose were handled proactively and professionally.

Phew! I'm glad we are through that: The case study could finish here. A turbulent period of change had been managed well and no-one could criticise the executive team in Dublin if they took a well-earned rest. What nobody knew at that time was that the next tidal wave of change was about to hit the shore. Lucent Technologies came knocking at the door.

CHANGE YOUR PLACES AGAIN: LUCENT DESCENDS ON ASCEND

Lucent Technologies was born in the break-up of the AT&T organisation in the USA. While only 'legally' four years old, the company had a 100+ year history. Headquartered in New Jersey, Lucent employed over 150,000 people and had become a central player across several industries, majoring in telecommunications (mobile phones, internet access, telephone exchanges and telephone manufacturing). The company had an R&D reputation and bench strength that was unmatched, boasting more Nobel Laureates than any other commercial organisation on the planet. Alexander Graham Bell had invented the telephone; he also left a legacy for both pure and applied research that led AT&T to develop a slew of breakthrough products including lasers, the integrated circuit (IC) and even an understanding of how the earth was formed (the so-called 'big bang' theory). The company had an ocean-deep reputation for research and design producing a diverse range of products.

Lucent's 'crosshairs' had settled over Ascend Communications because of its product portfolio. This was not difficult to understand; both company's products had massive overlap. However, what was difficult to fathom was the *speed* of execution. When asked about a possible Lucent acquisition some months earlier, one senior executive remarked, "It will be two years before they find our telephone number". As a $100 billion dollar giant organisation, Lucent was not known for being 'fleet of foot'. But, things were changing.

We want to expand: Should We Grow or Buy?

In simple terms, there are two ways to expand a business, grow or buy. Lucent demonstrated an almost 'insatiable buy' appetite with a range of purchases over a 15-month period. On 23 July 1999, the official 'sign-off' took place and Ascend formally became part of Lucent. The purchase price was $24bn —a reflection of Ascend's $1.2 billion annual sales and 60% annual growth rate. These were heady days.

Separating the 'Excellence' from the 'Stretch' Agenda

As the relationship with Lucent began to develop, an ever-increasing amount of executive time was being 'sucked into' managing this new, complex international relationship. The Ascend Communications business was folded into the INS (InterNetworking Systems) division in Lucent and the debates began around how Dublin could support the strategic growth of this part of the company. The question was complicated by a second possibility — should the Dublin site support the 'other' businesses in Lucent?

In simple terms, Lucent was split into four separate businesses:

INS (Inter Networking System)	ONG (Optical Business)	Wireless	SSG Switching Solutions Group (TELCO)

Historically, each of these sectors within the company had dedicated manufacturing plants, offering a high degree of self-sufficiency. However, the drive in subsidiary businesses for self-sufficiency needs to be balanced against the organisational principle of cost-effectiveness. A simple analogy may illustrate this point. If there are 10 carpenters on a building site, each will want to have their own power drill. However, at any moment in time, it is unlikely that all 10 drills are being used. It follows that the principle of self-sufficiency (best for each individual) needs to be balanced against the counterprinciple of asset utilisation (best for the organisation).

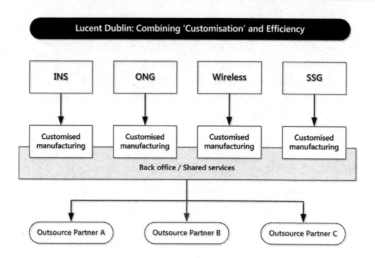

While Dublin was clearly part of the INS division, it was left open to the executive team in Dublin to make contact with senior executives in other divisions to 'sell' the idea of locating in Ireland. Could the four central 'business sectors' in Lucent become 'product design houses' with their 'Operations' being managed centrally through Dublin? An attempt to capture this idea diagrammatically is outlined above.

If the Irish site could handle the outsourcing of manufacturing for INS (which also had manufacturing facilities in Germany and Spain), could this be replicated for the other sectors under the Lucent umbrella? The outcome of this debate would be hugely important to the Dublin operation. For example, if the optical business decided to establish an operation in Ireland, this would mean the construction of a new manufacturing facility, the recruitment of hundreds of new people and a potential revenue stream of US$1 billion from this business alone. In fact, the Dublin plant had expanded its relationships with external contractors and now had a range of possibilities on offer (see below).

The 'fogginess' around these major business decisions was made more complex by several changes in senior personnel within Lucent. As there are few 'absolutes' in this area, a change in personnel could turn a decision 180° and the 'Dublin position' changed several times over a turbulent six-month period.

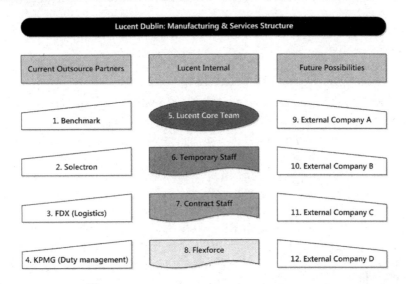

Growing Dissatisfaction among the Middle Management Team

While the various scenarios were playing out at the senior level, in Dublin a growing dissatisfaction in the middle management ranks was becoming apparent. Confused about the company mission (*what business are we in*) the middle management team felt that the senior group were 'taking their eye off the ball' – paying too much attention to the *tomorrow* agenda and ignoring *today*. The ambiguity about the company's future had lent itself to some intensive debates among the senior team in Dublin. As an external consultant, I had facilitated a number of these events, temporarily entering the same 'confused space' that the executive team inhabited on a day-to-day basis.

Some of these debates were *robust* and relationships were becoming strained in a highly pressurised, uncertain environment. Following one internal meeting that had been particularly confusing, one of the key mid-level managers made an appointment to see Eoin O'Driscoll. In a 60-minute, no-holds-barred meeting, the picture painted was stark. Basic plant disciplines were beginning to slip; the senior team were struggling to manage with 'too many balls in the air'. Tensions around performance slippages were leading to the emergence of a 'blame culture' in which the search for the guilty was taking precedence over the search for root causes or solutions. There was a strong sense that some of the most talented managers were disaffected – considering moving to new pastures – where the 'fog' was less dense and work pressures less intense. Something had to be done, soon.

The Excellence Agenda Moves to Centre Stage

The solution chosen was to 'split' the management agenda into two component parts: a *today* (excellence) and a *tomorrow* (stretch) agenda. All day-to-day plant issues would be managed against the 'excellence' agenda. The logic: regardless of which strategic decision was made about the Dublin plant, manufacturing systems needed to be maintained at gold-medal standard. The second line management team was empowered to develop this concept into a workable set of projects, with defined metrics and a management process that would keep it all on track. These projects were split into two 'groups': *Immediate Issues* that needed to be resolved in the short term *(crocodiles to be shot in the next 30 days)* and *Critical Success Factors* – what needed to be in place to create the best managed manufacturing facility anywhere in Lucent. The central underlying issues, along with a 'structure' to deliver against these, were developed at a two-day off site meeting that I facilitated. The entire middle-management team attended and we worked out the mechanics of the excellence agenda in some detail. In later meetings, the fine-grained details of how the excellence agenda would be managed were finalised. It was the latest initiative as the company moved into this new phase.

The 'Stretch' Agenda is Given Proper Air Time

In parallel with the excellence initiative, the executive team in Dublin began to craft the 'stretch' agenda. They developed a range of possible options/scenarios in order to be able to respond to requests from the US, a moving target. The goal: to maximise the contribution of the Dublin operation, subject to doing what was right for the Lucent Corporation – a core decision was made that the 'national agenda' would not override corporate interests. In theory, it might be possible to convince some senior executive to locate a new venture in Dublin – but this would only be done if it made more sense than locating it in Singapore or somewhere else. This was less altruism than pragmatism. The senior executives in the US had not been elevated without having the smarts to see quickly through any narrow sectional interests. Playing it 'straight' made life simpler, more authentic and was more likely to yield a successful outcome. The excellence and stretch agendas were managed side-by-side with clearly defined responsibilities for each group. Later, as the excellence agenda issues were documented and better understood, they would be 'folded in' to people's core work objectives — becoming part of the 'day job' rather than a stand-alone set of projects. Complexity understood and managed. Another brick in the wall.

Looking Ahead: Key 'Going forward' Issues to be managed

At that point, I began to work with the senior team to look further ahead – through the windscreen – to envisage the type of issues that might emerge. Key organisational challenges at that point included:

- **Lightning Speed: Could Lucent Use Time as a Competitive Weapon?** From its AT&T legacy, Lucent inherited a fully integrated business model with all of the needed resources under its direct control. Yet the question remained whether Lucent would have the 'organisational agility' to manage in this faster-paced environment? The navigational skills required to pilot an oil tanker are different to a speedboat. Managing in 'internet-time' is fundamentally different to traditional businesses where most senior managers 'served their apprenticeship'. While undoubtedly managing in this fast-paced environment can be 'learned', some large organisations are held back by their DNA; success in a particular environment does not automatically translate into success in the new economy. The rules of the two games are contradictory. Because of its particular history in the 'slower' AT&T days, there was a genuine question around whether Lucent could compete in an environment where time is a competitive weapon.

- **Could the Potential of the Irish Site be Fully Exploited?** The core capability of the Irish operation was in the ability to manage a diverse range of manufacturing/service opportunities tax-effectively. Part of the skill in exploiting this was around the political savvy in moving manufacturing capability into an unconventional outsourced model. Critics of multi-nationals often portray large companies as pursing economic interest above all else. The reality of life in this sector is that decisions are made based on a combination of economics, personal politics and national loyalty. Relocating production to a new geographical area has to overcome very real opposition to this — from established manufacturing facilities in the same company. The success of the Irish operation in establishing service level agreements that actually worked, developing skills in manufacturing engineering and competence in new product introduction (NPI) augured well for future success.

- **Winning the People War: Creating 'Sticky' Talent in Ireland:** That there are 1,300+ multinational organisations operating in Ireland is testament to a range of government initiatives (tax, infrastructure, subsidies, international marketing) that underpinned economic management. However, the Celtic Tiger years put huge pressure on available management and specialist talent — which the net immigration of Irish managers and import of talented overseas executives was barely able to overcome. During the timelines for this case, unemployment in Ireland stood at 4.5%, less than half the EU average (these numbers seem amazing now). Realistically, this is 'full employment'. It follows that part of the company's success going forward would be in creating 'sticky talent' — key people who are super-glued to the organisation on the basis of opportunity for personal and financial growth. Inevitably, a lot of the senior executives' time to date in Dublin had been 'outwardly' focused. It was now time to begin to build a 'Lucent tribe' — incorporating the best elements of the Stratus culture into the new operation.

- **Exploiting the depth of Lucent's Global R&D expertise:** At the corporate level, Lucent is rich in R&D talent with some 30,000+ researchers, 4,000 of whom have *multiple PhDs*. For all multi-nationals, a continuing challenge is to 'connect the parts' – to ensure that functional expertise is cross-pollinated across the organisation. How the company would ensure that the R&D 'talent' finds its way into practical manufacturing solutions was a key challenge posed. One idea was to relocate some of this R&D expertise nearer to the 'front line'. But, as one manager stated wryly: "Not every genius wants to live in New Jersey".

This superbly-managed organisation demonstrated how to cope with change in a white-water, turbulent environment and is a brilliant example of 'agile responding'. In the words of Damon Runyon, the author of *Guys & Dolls*: 'The race is not always to the swift, nor the battle to the strong, but that's the way to bet'.

PAUL MOONEY

Paul Mooney holds a Ph.D. and a Post-Graduate Diploma in Industrial Sociology from Trinity College Dublin, along with a National Diploma in Industrial Relations (Distinction) from the National College of Ireland. Paul is a Fellow of the Chartered Institute of Personnel and Development and is widely recognised as an expert on organisation and individual change.

Paul began his working life as a butcher in Dublin. After completing a formal apprenticeship, he moved into production management. He subsequently joined General Electric and held a number of human resource positions in manufacturing. After GE, Paul worked with Sterling Drug in Ireland and the Pacific Rim, with responsibility for all personnel activity across South East Asia.

On his return to Ireland, he established a management consulting company specialising in providing clients with customised Organisation and Management Development solutions. Between 2007 and 2010, Paul held the position of President, National College of Ireland. He then moved back into the consulting arena, setting up Tandem Consulting, a team of senior organisation development and change specialists. Paul has run consulting assignments in 20+ countries.

Paul's areas of expertise include:

- Organisational Development/Change & Conflict Resolution.
- Leadership Development/Executive Coaching.
- Human Resource Management/Employee Engagement.

For more information, check out Paul's blog *Confessions of a Consultant* at http://tandemconsulting.wordpress.com.

BOOKS BY PAUL MOONEY

Amie: The True Story of Adoption in Asia (1990)

Developing the High Performance Organisation (1996)

The Effective Consultant (1999)

Keeping Your Best Staff: The Human Resources Challenge (1999)

Turbo Charging the HR Function (2001)

The Badger Ruse (2004)

Union Free: Creating a Committed & Competent Workforce (2005)

Desperate Executives: Coaching, Change & Personal Growth (2007)

Accidental Leadership: A Personal Journey (2009)

The Transformation Roadmap: Accelerating Organisation Change (2012)

OAK TREE PRESS

Oak Tree Press develops and delivers information, advice and resources for entrepreneurs and managers. It is Ireland's leading business book publisher, with an unrivalled reputation for quality titles across business, management, HR, law, marketing and enterprise topics. NuBooks is its recently-launched imprint, publishing short, focused ebooks for busy entrepreneurs and managers.

In addition, through its founder and managing director, Brian O'Kane, Oak Tree Press occupies a unique position in start-up and small business support in Ireland through its standard-setting titles, as well as training courses, mentoring and advisory services.

Oak Tree Press is comfortable across a range of communication media – print, web and training, focusing always on the effective communication of business information.

Oak Tree Press, 19 Rutland Street, Cork, Ireland.

T: + 353 21 4313855 F: + 353 21 4313496.

E: info@oaktreepress.com W: www.oaktreepress.com.